Publisher
Theresa Murtha

Editor
Nancy Mikhail

Managing Editor
Michael Cunningham

Production Editor
Mark Enochs

Cover Designer
Michael Freeland

Illustrator
Judd Winick

Designer
Kim Scott

Indexer
Chris Wilcox

Production Team
Angela Calvert
Tricia Flodder
Megan Wade
Christy Wagner
Karen Walsh

Contents at a Glance

Contents

Part 3: Standard Rules and Guidelines   79

10 Grammar   81

11 Punctuation   87

12 General Style Issues   95

16 Memos   131

17 Email Messages   139

Foreword

Why is it that so many of us have trouble writing? You can see it in our behavior: we will undergo any torture short of brain surgery to squirm out of an assignment; then we procrastinate until the very last possible moment; and, when finally at work, we whine piteously to anyone who will listen about how hard writing is, how long it takes, and how nobody will read the final product anyway. Even professional writers like myself who have to write (or miss paying the mortgage) resort to pathetic stratagems to avoid the inevitable work. My own favorite ploy: claiming that I can't write until a necessary piece of software arrives from Calcutta or maybe Helsinki.

I have often wrestled with this question while driving along suburban streets, trolling down office hallways, and doing other things to avoid writing. The answer finally came to me one day when I was attending a kids' party (mostly to avoid writing something) at the local community center with a batch of other parents. The teacher had planned to accompany the children on the piano as they danced the Hokey-Pokey, but she had sprained her wrist earlier that day.

"Is there anyone here who can play the Hokey-Pokey?" she asked the parents.

Much to my surprise, several hands went up and after a few moments a reluctant dad stepped up to the keys and pounded out a serviceable rendition of the Hokey-Pokey. Suddenly for the first time in my life I realized that writing was like any other human activity—playing the piano, singing, swimming, cooking, or selling real estate. A few among us may become stars who will write best-selling novels, perform at the Met or the Olympics, dream up fabulous creations in chocolate, or make billions of dollars buying and selling skyscrapers. Some of us will only have enough ability to perform at a Bar Mitzvah, to make the varsity team in college, to run a catering business, or to sell houses in the neighborhood. Almost all of us, however, can learn enough of the basics to do all of these things—play the piano, sing a song, swim across a pool, cook dinner, and sell our own house—not perfectly, perhaps, but well.

If this is true, then, why are we so intimidated? The root of the problem seems to lie in the way we learn to write. Most of us learn (or, at least, are taught) the basics—how to write a sentence, how to punctuate, and so on—in grade school. As we advance, however, English teachers shift their focus from the drudgery of spelling and grammar to Great Literature. Supposedly, if we read tons of this stuff, the methods and inspiration of the great novelist or poet will somehow rub off on us or, by osmosis, become a part of our thinking. Then, we too will become artists capable of expressing all manner of subtle emotions and ferreting out the meaning of life and other big issues. Writing letters, reports, and other routine communications will somehow fall into place.

Now, I have nothing against Jane Austen or Walt Whitman or Mark Twain or any other literary giant. Nor do I think that any school child should avoid reading them. Nevertheless, it's unclear how much help the study of literature gives us in completing the writing tasks of everyday business life. After all, did Jane Austen ever have to write a manual to explain how to operate the new copying machines? Walt Whitman would have gone to pieces had he ever been required to write a proposal for a foundation grant, and Mark Twain's ability to draft a tactful memo about the shortcomings of the sales staff would probably have been nil. So we don't see any well-written communications that we can use as exemplars in our real lives. Worse yet, we come away from school with the notion that only the truly talented or divinely inspired can write. Most of us are pretty certain that we're not high and mighty artists; so we quake and quail even when drafting an email announcing a client meeting.

To succeed at the writing we do in business and elsewhere requires less art than craft, however. And, as we all know, craft can be learned. With some teaching, almost all of us can grasp enough of the basics to lay bricks, bake a cake, play a simple tune on the piano, sew a seam, fix a carburetor, and play tennis. With lots of practice, many of us could probably even aspire to do all those things terrifically. And, so it goes with writing. It is a craft like any other. Master the techniques, and, true, you won't be Shakespeare, but you might be a terrific business writer.

Teaching that craft is the aim Marcia Layton has set in *The Complete Idiot's Guide to Terrific Business Writing*. Calling on her experience as a public relations professional, she lays out what she's learned in a way that will be useful to business people who must produce what I call "prose with a purpose." She reveals the most helpful techniques for good writing and explains how to avoid and correct the most common mistakes made by business writers. She guides us through data collection and organization in which we often get mired for months on end and explains how to get from that morass to a good first draft. She also identifies the many and various forms of business communications—letters, reports, email, press releases—and offers tips for success with each.

More important than all those lessons, however, may be Marcia Layton's overriding message: that we can all learn to write and write well. Indeed, by following her principles, we may be able to banish forever the notion that writing is just another one of those things that we can't do. With her help, we can do it and do it well.

Marlys Harris

Columnist for *Money Magazine* ("Money Helps" column) and for *Family Life* ("Family Strategies" column).

Introduction

If you find yourself trying to avoid any type of writing assignment—from thank you letters to full-blown proposals—you're going to love *The Complete Idiot's Guide to Terrific Business Writing*.

Written for people who think they can't write or who have been scared off by memories of high school English classes, this book helps you get over the fear of facing a writing project. It will also help you learn exactly how to put together common documents, such as letters, memos, proposals, and even press releases. So even if you're not sure how to write a report—you'll learn!

In Part 1, "How to Become a Better Writer," you'll see writing in a whole new light. Instead of being difficult and tedious, you'll learn how to make writing fun and easy.

Part 2, "Getting Started," gets to the heart of writing a document, providing specific steps for creating a solid draft. You'll hear how to put together an outline and use it effectively, as well as how to organize all your thoughts.

Part 3, "Standard Rules and Guidelines," covers the basics of grammar, punctuation, and style issues to help build your technical skills. You need to know the rules so you're aware of when you're breaking them.

Part 4, "Presentation Basics," shows you how to make your documents look great. The words you write are crucial, but how they look on the page is sometimes equally important.

Part 5, "Common Types of Documents and Letters," teaches you how to prepare a wide range of typical business documents, from letters to proposals and reports. You'll be a pro in no time.

Extras

Because writing can get complex at times, friendly, easy-to-read tips are provided throughout the chapters to keep it interesting. Look for these symbols to find new ideas and suggestions:

Tips
These boxes offer helpful writing tidbits and advice on making sure your business correspondence gets read!

Quotes
These are quotations and suggestions from other writers on how they tackle writing problems.

Warnings
Putting something that doesn't belong in your letter, memo, or proposal or using incorrect grammar can send your one-of-a-kind business idea off someone's desk and straight into the trash can. Look in these boxes for advice on avoiding common errors.

Definitions
Using the right word can make or break you in the business world. Impress every-one with these literary terms, online terms, and general business phrases.

Acknowledgments

There are several people who were instrumental in making this book a reality and who deserve my sincere thanks. First, a thank you to Theresa Murtha and Megan Newman at Macmillan Publishing who gave me the chance to create this book.

Nancy Mikhail, my on-the-ball editor, kept me on track and improved the quality of the book immensely. Her help is greatly appreciated.

I am also grateful to Charlie Turner, the wonderful man in my life, who provided support and encouragement when I needed it most. Thank you.

Special Thanks from the Publisher to the Technical Reviewer

The Complete Idiot's Guide to Terrific Business Writing was reviewed by an expert who not only checked the technical accuracy of what you'll learn in this book, but also provided invaluable insight and suggestions to ensure that you learn everything you need to know when writing any type of business letter. Our special thanks are extended to:

Sheryl Lindsell-Roberts is a well-known and highly respected author who's been writing books for the professional market for the last fifteen years. Her first book, *The Office Professional's Quick Reference Handbook* is now in its fourth edition. Sheryl is also a freelance writer whose credits include marketing communications, training programs and seminars, reports, brochures, and user manuals. She has received national acclaim on nationwide talk shows and in several magazines including *Woman's Day*. Sheryl resides in Marlborough, Massachusettes with her husband Jon.

Part 1
How to Become a Better Writer

This part will help you understand exactly what good writing is, and how you can start to recognize it. You'll also learn common problems that writers encounter so that you can avoid them in your writing. Once you become a little more familiar with some basic rules of the English language, you can work on improving how to communicate in writing. And the more you do it, the better you'll get.

Chapter 1

What Is Good Writing?

In This Chapter

➤ The connection between good writing and good business

➤ Quantity vs. quality

➤ The elements of good writing

➤ Why you need to forget what you learned in school

Remember back in high school when a key part of each writing assignment was turning in a certain number of pages or words? It seemed that it mattered less what you said, as long as you said it in five pages. And if you said it in more than five pages, you were virtually guaranteed an A. The grading system implied that the more words you used, the better the quality of writing.

Unfortunately, after spending so much time learning those rules, you need to forget a lot of them.

The rules of good business writing are sometimes the opposite of what you learned in school. Now, instead of shooting for quantity, you need to focus on quality. If you can make your point in one page, there's no need to write four. And if you write more than is necessary, people won't think more of your writing—they may not even read it. In a sense, you will have failed.

Good Writing Skills and Your Career

While doing a good job plays a big role in moving up the career ladder, being a good communicator is also essential to success in business. Writing and speaking well can be the difference between getting promoted or not.

In 1982 a group of researchers asked newly promoted U.S. executives which of 13 courses, including the common business courses, best prepare a person for a career in general management. Business communications, written and oral, was the course selected as more important than any other course, according to the *Journal of Education for Business*.

If you have an innovative solution to a problem your company has been facing, or if you've come across some interesting findings in a research project you've been working on, you need to be able to clearly explain those ideas to others.

Good writing requires a certain level of creativity to find the best way to express a thought or to make a point. Think about the creativity involved in writing a letter to sell a product to a group of clients; you have very little time to convince them that your product is the answer to their prayers.

> **Quote**
> The main mistake business writers make is in thinking formality and big words are better than simplicity.
>
> **Linda Stern**, a regular contributor to *Newsweek* and a syndicated personal finance coulmnist.

Or how about the creativity required to respond to letters from irate customers. You need to accomplish several things with your reply: Let them know you're sorry for their trouble, offer to fix whatever they're dissatisfied with, and thank them for taking the time to contact you. Careful wording can mean the difference between a happy customer who'll tell everyone how you promptly took care of his problem, or the even more angry customer who decides to initiate a class action suit. Communicating effectively can mean business success or failure.

The Difference Between Personal and Business Writing

When you write a letter to your dear Aunt Sally, your purpose is probably to fill her in on what you've been up to. Or maybe you need to thank her for the check she sent you on your birthday. Whatever the reason, when you write a personal letter you're addressing it to someone you know well. If your grammar isn't perfect or you don't spell every word correctly, nobody cares. Aunt Sally is going to love you just as much.

But there is a difference between writing for personal reasons and writing for business.

Personal correspondence is often handwritten, with an emphasis on keeping in touch with the recipient of your note. Letting your personality and style show through in your personal notes is encouraged, and often enjoyed by the recipient. Humor is great, as are expressions of affection.

This is not the case with business writing, however. Business writing is almost always undertaken for a specific purpose. There is an underlying mission with business writing that just isn't there with personal writing, and you need to be aware of the difference.

Correspondence in business is typically used to communicate corporate news, report on progress toward company goals, or persuade customers to buy more of your company's products or services.

In business, you often don't know all the people who will eventually read what you've written. So you need to be sure you follow the dos and don'ts of business writing that we'll go through shortly.

What Characterizes Good Writing?

In some ways, it's difficult to define exactly what good writing is. It's obvious when we come across something that has been written poorly, but something that's good is harder to identify.

➤ Good writing sounds natural, not overdone or confusing. The writer sounds as if he is speaking directly to you.

➤ It is well organized, with one thought logically following the previous one. Each sentence builds on the one before it, leading you gradually to the conclusion.

Dos and Don'ts of Good Writing

You can improve your writing immediately if you follow some tips for better communication:

Dos

➤ Use the active voice, speaking directly to the reader:

Don't use: Gerald was given the award for employee of the month by Mr. Smith.

Rewrite this sentence so that the subject of your sentence is taking action, rather than having something done unto him.

Use: Mr. Smith awarded Gerald the employee of the month award.

➤ Vary the number of words in each sentence. If you're prone to run-on sentences that never end, read over what you've written and break up some of the sentences into shorter ones. Or if every sentence is 15 words long, try combining some here and there to keep it interesting.

➤ Vary the number of sentences in your paragraphs. If all of your paragraphs are three sentences long, the reader settles into a reading pace that becomes boring after a while. Having some paragraphs with two sentences, some with five, and maybe some with just a single sentence helps keep the reader engaged.

Definition
Bullet Points Those little round dots that appear before sentences. They look like this (•) and are often used in place of numbers or hyphens.

Definition
Heading A short phrase that summarizes the key point discussed in a section or paragraph. It usually appears immediately above the section. An example of a heading is:

VACATION HOLIDAY SCHEDULE ABC Company will celebrate the following holidays during 1997:

➤ Emphasize a positive message whenever possible, instead of a negative. For instance, if you need to report to employees that they'll need to work overtime during the holidays, point out the amount of extra money they will make rather than the less time they'll have to spend at home.

➤ Use correct grammar and spelling. Nothing ruins a well-expressed opinion more than an incorrectly spelled word or poor grammar. Your abilities as a writer will be questioned as the number of mistakes pile up. Correct word and spelling usage should be a given in all your writing. (Spell- and grammar-check programs on your computer can be a *big* help in this regard.)

➤ Be sure that your document is visually appealing. If you've used teeny, tiny print that fills 99% of the white space on the page, people are going to avoid reading whatever you've written. We'll get into some formatting basics later, but in general, use things such as bullet points to break up a long list of items. Headings are also useful before each major section to let people know what they'll read about.

➤ Keep your readers' interest in mind. Remind yourself constantly of why people are reading this document. What do they expect to learn from you? What's the point of what you're writing?

Don'ts

➤ Don't use more words than necessary to make a point. Wordiness only shows that you're not really sure of what your point is.

➤ Don't try to be humorous. Being funny is very difficult and usually fails. Even if you were the class clown, you can't be sure that everyone is going to appreciate what you think is funny. It's safer to work for professionalism in your writing, rather than for laughs.

➤ Don't use jargon and slang. Unless you are sure of exactly who will be reading your writing, it's better not to use words that will only be understood by a small group of people. Physicians writing for the *New England Journal of Medicine* use medical lingo and scientific terms because they know that nearly everyone reading their report is part of the medical community.

But if you wrote an article on the new technology used in your company's newest product for a business magazine, only readers with a technical background would understand what the heck you were talking about. It's smarter to leave technical terms and business buzzwords out of your writing.

Don't overuse slang. When writing becomes too colloquial, it starts to look sloppy and unpolished.

➤ Don't use sexist language. Granted, it's difficult to know how to write without offending someone. But it's better to weave in references to "she" and "her" whenever possible, so you don't seem to be leaving women out of your discussion. Keep in mind that both men and women will be reading your writing, so try to include them both in any documents you write.

Tip
When in doubt, leave it out.

And when writing letters, don't assume that a man will be the one receiving it. Find out whether the recipient is a man or a woman so you'll know whether to write "Mr. Smith" or "Ms. Smith." Or if you're not sure, it's better to send it to "Dear J. Jones" rather than "Mr./Ms. Jones" or, worse yet, "Dear Gentleman."

➤ Don't use clichés. Using phrases and silly jokes that have been around forever just make your writing seem stale. Even if there's a cliché that would be perfect for the letter or report you're working on, come up with a different way of making the same point.

Definition
Colloquial
An informal, conversational style that is generally not appropriate for business documents.

Forgetting Old Rules

You may have had the following rules drummed into your head during grade school, but now you have to forget them. You were probably told repeatedly:

➤ Never end a sentence with a preposition. This is generally a good rule to follow, but if it makes your writing sound stiff or unnatural, forget it.

For example, which of the following sentences sounds better?

1. His constant lateness was something she would not put up with.

2. His consistent lateness was something up with which she would not put.

➤ Never begin a sentence with "and" or "but." If you're writing an article for a newspaper or magazine, stick with this rule. However, sometimes it just sounds better to use one of these two words to split a sentence that's too long to provide supporting information for a point you just made.

➤ Sentence fragments—sentences without both a noun and a verb, or without a complete thought—are not real sentences. Well, in this day and age, sometimes they are, such as when a sentence fragment immediately follows a complete sentence to emphasize the central point.

Here is an example of a sentence fragment at work:

Do you think you can't afford a new car? You can! 1996 was a good year for XYZ Company. A really good year.

How You Can Become a Better Writer

Besides following the general rules of grammar, spelling, and punctuation, which we'll cover later, keep these points in mind:

➤ **Let your readers know right away why you're writing, preferably, in the first paragraph.** What is the point of the document they're reading? Is it a report on the findings of the research project you've been working on? Is it your recommendations for changes to the structure of your organization? Is it a performance appraisal of one of your staff members? Don't make readers try to figure out why they have your document in their hands—tell them up front.

The inverted pyramid technique, which many of us were taught in high school writing, is still a smart concept to follow. In an inverted pyramid, you make a general statement first and then get more and more specific in subsequent sentences, supporting your original statement. You can think of your whole document as an inverted pyramid, as well as the individual paragraphs in your document. Each one can be started with a general statement that is followed by supporting information.

➤ **Brevity is a virtue.** Work to keep your writing concise, clear, and as short as possible. Of course, if you're preparing a government grant proposal, it will probably need to be 50 pages or more. But if it only needs to be 50 pages, turn in 50, not 75 or 100. Quantity will not score you bonus points in business.

Quote
If I have to read a sentence or para-graph a second time to get its meaning, the writer may lose me. Keep sentences short and limited to one major point.

Deborah Layton, Senior Associate Diretor of Planned Giving at the University of Pennsylvania (and my mom).

The Least You Need to Know

➤ A large percentage of your competence on the job is measured by your writing abilities.

➤ Quantity does not equal quality in business writing. Excess verbage wastes everyone's time.

➤ Forget those stodgy rules you learned in grade school and write the way you talk, so that you sound more natural.

➤ Keep your readers' interests in mind at all times so that your writing is to the point and concise.

It was a dark and stormy night...

Chapter 2

Avoiding Common Writing Problems

In This Chapter

➤ Getting past boring writing

➤ Choosing your words carefully

➤ Staying focused on your purpose

➤ Speaking *to* your readers—not down at them

➤ Using a positive tone—not a negative one

While good writing is often hard to define, bad writing is pretty obvious. You know it when you see it because it's hard to understand, boring, lengthy, or all of the above.

Some of the common problems that crop up regularly are easy to spot. And since they're so obvious, they should also be easier to avoid.

How Cliché

Clichés are those phrases you've heard so many times that you almost don't see them when you read them. I'm sure you've heard at least one of the following:

➤ "He can't see the forest for the trees."

➤ "Six of one, half a dozen of the other."

➤ "She sees the glass as half-empty, instead of half-full."

Although everyone knows what you mean when you use a cliché, you're also not expressing anything new. Your thought or idea, revolutionary or not, is going to come across sounding like something your audience has heard a hundred times before.

Clichés aren't forbidden, but they should be used in moderation. You can go overboard with clichés and turn your audience off. Throwing in one cliché after the other is not a good idea. The solution is to find a different way to get your point across whenever possible. After you finish writing your proposal, report, letter, or press release, read through it again in search of clichés. When you come across one, think about the point you were trying to make. Then rewrite the sentence a new way to communicate your idea without the cliché.

Of course, there are those situations where a cliché just sums up your point nicely. That is the time when you should feel free to use one.

Restating the Obvious

Being concise and clear is extremely important in business writing. You can't ramble on and waste the reader's time; there are too many other memos to be seen or proposals to be reviewed. So once you've made your point, move on to the next issue you want to address, or to use a cliché, don't beat a dead horse.

Quote
Treat your readers as if they are busy, smart, and completely uninformed about the subject of your work.

Linda Stern, a regular contributor to *Newsweek* and *Home Office Computing*.

Saying the same thing several ways just isn't smart. In addition to taking twice as long to read, it also suggests that you don't think the reader is bright enough to have gotten your point the first time around. It can appear insulting.

One of the best ways to avoid redundancy is to organize your thoughts up front. Before you start to write, think through all the different points you want to make, or areas you need to address. Whether you're writing a brief memo, personnel letter, or new business proposal, you'll want to make sure you touch on every important item.

Once you've identified the key issues to write about, put them in order from most important to least important. Prioritize. Then start writing by filling in the details. Why is that first point so crucial? What is it that your client doesn't realize about your com-petitor's quote? How is it that your recommendations provide the best solution? Whatever the points are that you want to raise, go through them one by one in your writing.

The key here is that once you've said what you need to say, don't bring up that same point again later. Keep all the relevant information in its own little section. Don't let it spread into other parts of your letter or proposal. That's when your writing becomes redundant and irritating.

Sounding Overbearing

No one likes a know-it-all. You know, those people who seem to lecture you, rather than have a two-way conversation with you. They prefer talking to listening and seem to feel that what they have to say is more important than anything you might want to add.

Well, the same way that someone can grate on your nerves in conversation can also turn you off to his or her writing.

An overbearing tone comes through as arrogant; as though the writer feels that she is superior in some way. Instead of sharing information or expressing a thought, the writer now comes across as very patronizing. Few people I know like to be talked down to, which is what an overbearing tone sounds like.

Your writing sounds overbearing if you seem to assume that the person reading your letter or pro-posal knows less than you do. If you constantly define words, explain details, or feel it necessary to give overly simplistic examples, someone reading what you've written may become offended or turned off. One way to get around that, or at least make your words seem less arrogant, is to make your audience feel that they are equals. Use the word "we" to include your audience in your thought process, rather than creating an "us" and "them" scenario.

Tip
Sometimes beginning a statement with, "as we all know..." provides a nice way of putting everyone on equal footing. Even if we don't all know, using inclusive phrases like this shows your reader that you think of him as being just as qualified as you are. Similar openings are "I'm sure you've heard..." or "you are probably aware that..."

You can also offer your opinion or recommenda-tions, but don't make it seem as if they are the only ones in town worth listening to (even if you are absolutely sure that's the case). Your reward for showing respect for your reader is that he will be more apt to support your recommendations, back your proposals, and respond approvingly to any letters you might write or memos you decide to distribute.

Success in business is often linked to communication abilities. In addition, the way that you communicate can significantly affect your relationships with co-workers, bosses, and mentors. Keep these points in mind as you put together your next memo.

Overbearing writers also sound negative, which isn't good. Maintaining a positive writing style and attitude has a major impact on your reader and leaves them feeling good about what they've read. This doesn't mean that you always have to turn bad news into good news; it just means that you should try to communicate a positive attitude or tone.

To do that, avoid criticizing people or projects in your writing. That only sets a negative tone. You can point out areas for improvement, but you'll get more support if you stay away from complaining or whining.

Having an upbeat attitude means that you may point out situations that need fixing, but that you also don't dwell on the negative. You move on to mention good things that are happening, too. Or look to the future when the problems at hand will be corrected.

Communicating in an optimistic or positive tone makes your reader want to read on, rather than scaring them away or making them mad. And one measure of whether you're a successful writer is whether people bother to finish your memos or letters.

Getting Off Track

Sticking to the point you are trying to make can be tough. Especially if you write a lengthy document where you try to explain complex or involved situations. It's easy to get sidetracked into discussing issues that really don't matter.

Tangents are what we call those places writers go when they get off track. Instead of staying focused on the main issue being discussed, they digress. New, but sort of related, points are brought up and addressed. If you remember high school geometry, you can probably picture those lines that go off into different directions from the center; those are tangents.

Again, the solution to eliminating irrelevant material is to plan ahead. Lay out all the points you're going to discuss and then stick to the plan. Don't bring up this interesting, but non-essential, fact about such-and-such. Few people will care. They just want the major points.

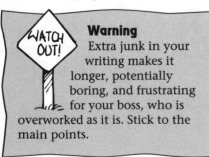

Warning
Extra junk in your writing makes it longer, potentially boring, and frustrating for your boss, who is overworked as it is. Stick to the main points.

You don't get extra points for trivia. Actually, you get penalized.

When you've finished writing something, set it aside overnight and reread it in the morning. Keep an eye out for extraneous material that doesn't relate to your most important material. If it can be deleted, delete it. Edit to make your writing as clear-cut as possible. Anyone reading your information will appreciate your "cutting to the chase."

Biases and Assumptions

People have their own personal biases or perspectives that they bring to their writing. Based on your upbringing and experiences you may believe certain things to be true that others, with different backgrounds, don't agree with.

While these differences are part of what makes America great, they can also be divisive. And you need to be aware of this when you're stating your own opinion, rather than sticking to the facts at hand. In addition to looking stupid, you could also offend a lot of people. Not a good career move.

Biases and Prejudices

When you believe something to be true, without any kind of proof or direct experience, you may be biased. Generally this applies more to beliefs about people and situations than anything else.

For instance, if you believe that Americans are smarter than people from any other country, that is a bias. You feel that certain people, from the U.S. for example, are superior in one way or another to people from other countries. But, of course, you have little proof of this, just your own personal belief. You are biased because you tend to favor one group over another.

Of course, you can also be biased in business toward a particular solution someone has presented in response to a problem that has come up. In this case, your bias is really a preference. You have a favorite method or answer.

Being prejudiced is similar to being biased. Prejudices are usually related to a group of people, rather than things or events, and suggest that some people are not as good as other people. While a bias suggests a preference for something, being prejudiced infers a dislike or preference against something. Both biases and prejudices are similar in that the beliefs being held are subjective and based on faulty information.

To keep biases and prejudices out of your writing, make sure that statements you make are factual or can be supported by some kind of evidence or proof. For example, writing a statement discouraging the introduction of a newsletter because you don't think that assembly-line personnel have adequate reading skills is clearly a prejudice. You have no information that suggests that those employees lack certain skills, you just have your own personal opinion.

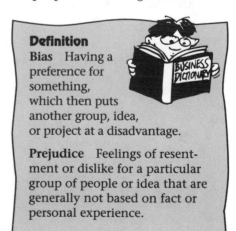

Definition

Bias Having a preference for something, which then puts another group, idea, or project at a disadvantage.

Prejudice Feelings of resentment or dislike for a particular group of people or idea that are generally not based on fact or personal experience.

Reread everything you've written to sort out which statements are your own opinions that you can support with evidence and which are statements that simply can't be supported. Those sentences and phrases should be deleted or replaced.

Assumptions

Biases and prejudices are based on assumptions—personal beliefs we hold that may or may not be true. The problem with assumptions is that they are based on each individual's life experiences, which is different for everyone. And different experiences and assumptions are often going to lead people to different conclusions.

What you have to watch out for in your writing is making statements based on your own assumptions, believing that everyone else is thinking the same way. Rarely does that happen.

Assumptions can make your writing hard to follow, or insulting to people who don't agree with you. They introduce an element of personal opinion when business writing should rely heavily on facts and analysis. When you state a reason for something, it should be based more on what is good for business than anything else. In many ways, your personal opinion and assumptions have no place in business writing.

To keep your writing free of implied assumptions, constantly ask yourself as you write, "Why do I believe this statement to be true?" If you ever find yourself answering, "Just because," or something to that effect, you know you're on to an assumption. To fix it, delete your assumption and replace it with a statement that can be supported by facts, reports from others, or an opinion that you can fully explain.

Mixed Metaphors

Metaphors are like symbols in writing—you use one word or phrase to mean another. Although metaphors are not used everyday in business, they are useful for explaining new concepts or situations to people. However, when they are used incorrectly they stand out like a black eye, which is why you need to be aware of the right way to use them in your own writing.

Tip
Similes are a lot like metaphors. The difference is that when you say something is *like* something else, you're using a simile. When you say that something *is* something else, you're using a metaphor.

In most high school English classes, we read books that have a lot of symbolism. If you've ever read Ernest Hemingway's *The Old Man and the Sea*, you may remember how there was a second meaning to almost every character or situation introduced in the book. Even the way the man walked referred to some other dimension and meaning.

Symbolism adds a second level, or new meaning, to writing. But it typically doesn't come into play in business writing. Rarely would you say something like "our balance sheet is a tree ready to bear fruit." But you might hear "we're on a sinking ship" if things aren't going too well at your company. Of course, you know that your building is land-locked and there's no way you're on a ship at all, but the image helps you see your company's situation in a new light. Metaphors can help to clarify things by relating them to situations you're very familiar with (you know that a sinking ship would not be a good place to be, for instance).

But metaphors can also cause problems when used improperly. That is, when you relate your situation to another that is the opposite of, or just different from, what you're experiencing, it can get confusing.

For instance, if you wrote that the management team at your competition is a pack of wild animals, what does that mean? You've used a metaphor, but it doesn't help anyone understand whether the management team is a threat or not. Is a pack of wild animals good or bad? It's hard to tell. That's a mixed metaphor.

The key in using metaphors correctly is making sure that the relationship you're trying to set up between one thing and another is parallel. The first person, place, situation, or thing you mention needs to be explained by the metaphor you use to describe it. And it needs to make sense.

Writing that "the board of directors meeting was a zoo" is good use of a metaphor because you give the reader a sense of what the atmosphere was like. In just one word you summarize how the meeting went, rather than describing who said what, who did what, and so on. All the connotations of a zoo help to give a better picture of what the meeting was like.

Imagine then if you said that "the board meeting was a lazy summer day." First of all, the pairing of meeting and day doesn't even sound alike. Both are nouns, but they aren't parallel at all. Envisioning a lazy summer day doesn't jibe with a meeting environment, so the metaphor doesn't work.

Using Technical Jargon, Legalese, and Phrases Only a Few Understand

When you use terms and words that only a few people are familiar with, you're being esoteric. Sometimes esoteric is OK, such as when you provide information to a small group of people who are the only people who would understand what you're talking about.

Using highly technical or industry-specific terms helps to save time when you're dealing with a group of people who understand such words. But if there is anyone in the group who is unfamiliar with what you're talking about, it might take more time to use and explain the technical terms than to speak in plain English.

If you write for a diverse audience, that is, a group of people who are from different departments, levels of education, or parts of your organization, you'll want to use words and phrases that you're sure everyone is familiar with. If you use highly technical terms when there are only a few technical people in the bunch, your writing will be ineffective; only a few people will understand you.

Tip
A thesaurus can be a big help in finding words that mean the same thing as the one you're used to using. Look for synonyms (words that mean the same thing as another), antonyms (words that mean the opposite of another word), and related words in a thesaurus.

Similarly, legal terms and phrases that are very formal should be avoided unless you are writing for a team of lawyers and judges. Legal mumbo jumbo tends to put people off and make them defensive. Since that's probably not the effect you want to have, you should stay away from terms usually used in a courtroom.

The best way 0to see if your writing will be understood by all is to have someone outside your department read your letter or memo before you send it out. If there are any words or phrases he hasn't seen before, you know which ones have to be taken out.

Buzzwords Galore

Buzzwords are those terms you hear almost daily within your company that are probably not in any dictionary. They are catchy phrases and sayings that are often trendy. When you use them, you let people around you know that you're on top of things; you're "in the know."

Tip
Some frequently used buzzwords, and their more common definitions in corporate America include:

Strategic alliance: Informal partnership

Downsized: Laid off or fired

Golden handcuffs: Salary, benefits, and perks that make it difficult to leave an organization

Paradigm: A pattern to how things are done

Frequently you'll find that your company has certain terms everyone uses that your friends in other organizations don't. In fact, they may never have heard them. But they probably have buzzwords everyone in their company uses that you've never heard either.

What this means is that you can use those terms, or buzzwords, internally, such as in memos and reports, but you should use them sparingly when writing for the outside world. Or, better yet, keep them out of proposals, letters, press releases, and external reports to be safe. You make customers and suppliers feel like outsiders, rather than an important part of your company's success, when you use words they don't know. So don't.

The Least You Need to Know

➤ Avoid redundancy and going off on tangents by jotting down all the ideas you want to get across first.

➤ Be sure you can back up recommendations and ideas with supporting facts, rather than just your own personal opinion. You don't want to appear biased or prejudiced.

➤ Metaphors and similes add color to your writing, but they can be tricky. When using these tools, be sure they help communicate your message, rather than making your writing more confusing.

➤ Don't use buzzwords or trendy phrases in documents going outside your company.

Whisper Whisper

REALLY?

Chapter 3

The Secret to Better Writing

In This Chapter

➤ How talking to a friend helps you write

➤ Why introductions can be deadly

➤ Supporting your point with evidence

➤ Staying focused on your message

So many people feel that they aren't good writers, or that they can't write at all. They find that it's a struggle to communicate what they want to say in words. If that describes you, don't give up. It will get easier. What most people in this situation need is simply practice. The more you write, the easier it is to get the words out the way you want. With time, you'll become more comfortable in expressing yourself.

Writing is kind of like running. It's so hard to get started but once you do, it's easy to keep going. You may start off gasping for air as your body warms up and gets used to moving at a faster pace. Then after about five minutes, you feel like you could run forever. The same is true of writing; once you get accustomed to putting words together, you'll be able to do it almost effortlessly.

Warning

WATCH OUT!

Don't struggle unnecessarily! Two handy writing tools that will make it much easier for you to find and correctly spell that perfect word are a dictionary and thesaurus. Also use a thesaurus to help you break out of the rut of using the same words repeatedly.

Write as if You Are Talking to a Friend

It's difficult to start writing when your audience consists of people you don't know. It's hard to imagine the committee that will review your report, or the potential client who will read your sales letter.

> **Quote**
>
> My advice to journalism students, back when I was teaching at a state university, was to "write the way you talk." Too many of my students would put on their writing hats and write in a stilted, imitative, or academic style.
>
> Put the reader in front of you (pick an actual person if you need to) and "speak" to them in writing. Then clean up any slang or grammatical errors and you have an easy, understandable, clear style.
>
> **Georgene Lockwood**, author of several books, including *Your Victorian Wedding: A Modern Guide for the Romantic Bride*.

When you're unfamiliar with your audience, you worry a lot about how your letter sounds. You may become concerned with the tone of voice you're using or whether you're providing too much or too little background information. This can really slow you down and bring on writer's block (see Chapter 9 if this happens).

Sometimes if you can't picture who you're writing to, it's tough to know what's going to interest them. This is important if, for instance, you're writing a sales letter trying to convince readers to buy your product. If you don't know what your readers are like, or what's important to them, it can be difficult to come up with some convincing selling points.

Tip
Talking to a friend makes it possible for you to imagine the type of person you're dealing with—someone intelligent and interested in your topic.

Try to think of someone you talk with or write to frequently. It can be a friend, colleague, or your mother. It doesn't matter who you think of—you just have to be able to visualize that person.

Once you've pictured your audience in your mind (let's say it's your friend, Fred), start explaining what you want to say as if you were talking to Fred. If you're proposing a cut in pay for the whole management team, for example, and you need to write a letter to the CEO recommending this step, pretend you're talking it over with your buddy. Since Fred doesn't know all that much about what's going on at your company, you'll need to start by giving him some background on the situation—why management needs to take a pay cut. Then explain why you believe that a pay cut is the answer. Since Fred, being the friend that he is, may suggest alternate solutions, you'll want to bring them up in your letter and address why they won't work as well as the solutions you're proposing.

Tip
You focus more on the message when talking with a friend. The result is that you make your point more clearly and concisely.

Simplicity and honesty are what you want to get across here. By pretending to talk over your situation with someone you're familiar with, you don't get as hung up over how it sounds. You tend to write as you talk, which sounds more natural and makes it faster to get the words out.

Get to the Point

Nothing is worse than reading a letter and wondering why the heck you received it in the first place. What was the point? What were you supposed to get out of it? In business, you need to state quickly why the person receiving information from you should take the time to read it. It's much better to get right to the point. Let them know the subject of your letter or memo immediately. After you've told them why you're writing, then you can start elaborating on the details.

In high school English, this first statement was frequently called a thesis statement. It's that one sentence that sets the tone for the rest of the document and explains right off the bat what the topic is.

Often your first sentence, or paragraph, is much like a thesis statement. You want your reader to know the point of your memo right away. Then you can start to elaborate and fill in some of the details.

For example, if you're issuing a memo to your company's security department regarding some new procedures for issuing ID badges, you might write something like this:

DATE: June 3, 1999

TO: Security Department

FROM: Jane Thompson

RE: New ID badges for vendors

Due to the need for suppliers and vendors to gain access to company facilities to meet with employees, we have designed a special vendor ID badge to be worn by all suppliers while on the premises.

After stating why you're sending out this memo, you can now get into the specifics of what the badge looks like, what it entitles the bearer to do, and how the staff should treat suppliers without ID badges.

Going from a specific statement to more general information helps you get right to the point.

Do You Really Need an Introduction?

What's almost equally aggravating is having to wade through a 15-page introduction just to get to the proposal itself. At that point, you should almost be done with the proposal, not just finishing the introduction.

Be very careful about using an introduction to anything you write. The danger is that you'll get so caught up in detailing background information that it will take pages and pages for you to get to the meat of the document. And your reader will be getting impatient. Or worse—bored.

If you feel the need to use an introduction, treat it as a chance to state what the current situation is that you'll address in your document. Use your introduction to quickly bring the reader up-to-speed. And the key word here is *quickly*.

Don't go overboard with historical information or details that aren't important at this point. Train yourself to constantly ask, "Does the reader really need to know this?" If the answer is ever "No," or "Probably not," then take the information out. This holds true for an introduction as well as the rest of the document. Keep any extraneous information out of your writing.

If you're writing an executive summary, which is often the first section of a longer document, keep in mind that the point of an executive summary is to distill many pages of information into one or two pages. Don't let it drag on and on.

Providing Supporting Evidence

Once you've told readers why you're writing, you've piqued their curiosity. You've given them just enough information to make them want to read on. That's where the supporting information comes in.

Supporting evidence consists of information about:

➤ Who

➤ What

➤ Where

➤ When

➤ How

"Why" is usually another aspect that is covered, but by this time, you've already told the reader why you're writing. Now move on to tell them about the other five elements.

Who

"Who" in the information you're writing up may be the management team of your company who've been asked to take that pay cut, or the group of assembly line personnel who've worked overtime during the past month to help introduce a new product, or maybe the 250 applicants who all applied for your one job opening.

It's possible that in your document, you won't need to write about anyone, but it's unlikely. Even if you're reporting on facts you've discovered, you'll still need to identify who was involved.

What

The "what" of your document is generally the subject that you're writing about.

In the first paragraph, you explained why you are writing; now you've got to elaborate about what the topic is. For instance, if you're writing a thank you letter to a vendor who performed above and beyond the call of duty, you'll want to talk about exactly what he did that was so exemplary. Did he complete a project in record time? Was the quality so far superior to what you've received from other vendors? Or was your representative extra attentive to your company's particular situation? Any and all of these reasons are the "what" aspect of your letter.

Other "what" angles include: what happened, what did someone do, what was sold, what was decided, or what was the problem.

Where

"Where" something occurred or will occur is frequently an important topic that you'll want to cover in your documents. Where deals with places.

If you're writing a press release announcing an upcoming press conference, you'll want to tell people where it is taking place so that the reporters know where to go. Or if you're writing a memo to your staff telling them to meet on Thursday for an important discussion, you'll want to tell them which room to meet in.

Sometimes, such as in a proposal to a client, where is not an important factor. But it's smart to run through all six factors—who, why, when, where, what, and how—to double-check.

When

If you're scheduling an event, "when" it is planned is important to report on. When refers to time, which can be the time of day a meeting is taking place, the date on which your report is due, or the year in which your company expects to go public.

How

"How" you're going to get something accomplished, such as meeting the terms of a contract your company just won, or persuading the president to give you a major raise, is another element to be addressed in your writing.

Be careful not to get too carried away with detailing how you'll complete something. Make sure the amount of information you're providing is ideal for the document you're writing.

For example, you don't want to explain every move you'll make or part you'll need in your quote to a potential customer. Their interest is more in the price and quality you'll provide, not how exactly you're going to put all the pieces together to make good on your widget contract.

On the other hand, a brief reference to the equipment your company has available to do the job should eliminate any concern the company may have about your ability to do the job.

Stay Focused

As you're filling in the details of your sales letter or press release, you may have a tendency to mention facts and trivia that really aren't necessary. This is only human.

We all tend to elaborate on stuff that we find interesting, whether the other person is interested or not. The solution is to try to constantly remind yourself of the reader's main interest or concern. What is the chief reason that you are writing this document? The answer to that question should guide you in staying on track.

For example, let's say you're writing a warning letter to an employee to let her know that if she continues to be late for work every day, she's going to be fired. The whole point of your letter is to get the employee to realize how serious her lateness is and that you won't let it continue. That's all.

So if she's also been disregarding other company policies, such as not following the dress code or smoking in the stairways, don't bring it up. You may be tempted to, just to let the employee know that you've noticed the other stuff, but don't. By bringing up other issues, such as the smoking or casual dress habits, you only take away emphasis from the main message: "Get to work on time!"

If you're just as upset about the way the employee is dressing or the fact that she's smoking in areas that she shouldn't be, write up separate warning letters to that effect. Don't lump everything together in one letter—write several if you really feel it's necessary. Think about the impact three separate warning letters will have on that employee, rather than one letter with a laundry list of things that she's doing wrong.

Tip
Keep your message simple and straightforward in order to ensure that the person receiving it understands exactly why you've written it.

This also holds true for very involved and lengthy reports, not just one-page letters. When you're preparing a report, the objective is to explain what was learned. And typically there is one area that is of greatest interest. That one area is the one that you want to stay focused on as you're writing up your report.

Tell a Story

You can always tell the difference between good and bad writing because good writing has a definite flow to it. You can clearly see the beginning, middle, and end with good writing. With bad writing, it's hard to follow where the writer is going.

One model to follow that will help you see if your writing has a beginning, middle, and end, is to pretend you're writing a story. All stories have a clear progression from one scene to the next. That's how your writing should come across—moving steadily from one point to the next without jumping all over the place.

Use Time as Your Guide

Sometimes a chronological order is best, providing information in the order in which it occurred. So if you're preparing a five-year strategic plan, first you'll talk about how the company has done in the past, then you'll describe the current situation, and then you'll address what the company plans to do in the future. The information is provided in a particular order, so that it makes sense to the reader.

If you were to write about the company's current situation, then go back and describe how the past was different, and finally zoom ahead and discuss what the future holds, your reader will be confused. It's often difficult to jump from one time frame to another and put everything into place. That's really the writer's responsibility.

The Inverted Pyramid

An inverted pyramid.

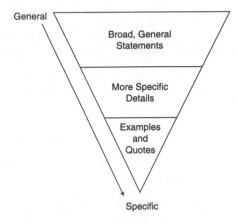

Another way to organize your information is from the most general to the most specific. This is called the inverted pyramid, because you write about the broadest subject first and get more and more specific as you write, so the flow of information looks like an inverted pyramid.

An example would be if you want to let employees know about changes to their insurance benefits. First, with the inverted pyramid format, you'd make a general statement to that effect, letting employees know that what they'll be reading about is their benefits package. Then, you'll get more and more specific about the changes, finishing with a description of the new plan.

The Pyramid

You can flip the inverted pyramid upside down by starting with the most specific statements and then moving on to more general ones.

In this case, describing the specific changes to the benefit plan first wouldn't work. If you started your memo with specific details and then got more general, employees would be confused. This is because you haven't told them up front what you're writing about.

But if you needed to alert employees to a particular incident that occurred, such as someone getting robbed in the parking lot, the pyramid format would work better. You would start with a statement describing what happened—the who, why, when, where, what, and how—to get everyone's attention and tell them right away why you are writing. Then you can generalize and provide suggestions on how employees can protect themselves from being robbed.

The best way to approach any document is to first write an outline to help determine which format will work best for you. You'll learn how to do that in Chapter 5.

The Least You Need to Know

➤ State up front why you are writing. Don't make it difficult for your reader to figure out what your point is.

➤ Pretend that you are telling your best friend what you're writing about. You'll feel more comfortable and be able to focus in on the key points you need to make.

➤ After stating the major point of your document, fill in the background details so that the reader understands "why."

➤ Good writing has a beginning, middle, and end, just like a story.

Part 2
Getting Started

Like anything, getting started on a project is often the most difficult part. Once you get underway, it doesn't seem so bad. But the trick is to get yourself moving.

This section will teach you how to put together an outline, write a first draft, and edit it. You'll also learn some techniques for combatting writer's block, which often hits at the worst possible time. With these tips, you'll be well on your way to writing with ease.

Chapter 4

Analyzing the Audience

In This Chapter

➤ "Who is my audience?"

➤ Your reader's background

➤ The role timing plays in your writing

➤ Editing your writing for different audiences

If you're under the impression that what you're writing about is the most important consideration in putting together your document, you're mistaken. Sure, the content of your message is crucial, but first you need to think about your audience. Who they are and what their needs are will guide how you write your document.

If you're unconvinced, think about this scenario: you're asked to prepare a report on your company's history of toxic emissions in the area. Pretty controversial subject, huh? OK, so what are you going to say? I'm not suggesting that you report different findings depending on who you're reporting to, just that you word things differently depending on whether your audience meets any of the following criteria:

➤ Has a scientific background and expects very specific technical data.

➤ Supports your company's efforts to reduce emissions and just wants a progress report.

➤ Hates your company and is pushing for it to relocate to Siberia.

➤ Is a team of doctors trying to determine whether there have been any medical problems as a result of the emissions.

You could certainly be writing for many other groups, but even with just those four examples, you can probably see how your audience will drastically affect the tone, level of detail, and length of your report.

Who Will Read What You Write?

"Who" is probably the key question when analyzing your reading audience. In order to picture them and to anticipate what they need to hear from you, you need to think about more specific issues, such as their level of responsibility, whether they are part of your organization or not, their attitude towards the subject you're addressing, and their level of familiarity with the topic.

Level of Responsibility

Within your organization, is the audience you're writing to above you, below you, or on the same level as you? Knowing this helps you gauge the tone and formality of your writing style.

Tip
Where your audience fits relative to you in the organizational structure will affect how you write your document.

Since your superiors have wider decision-making authority, you may want to approach communication with them more as a proposal, rather than as a mandate, which you might do with underlings.

With people at the same level as you, you'll probably provide recommendations. You can't force them to consider your ideas or points, but you can try to persuade them to see things your way.

Internal or External?

Communication within an organization is much less formal than letters and documents sent to people outside. You're providing information to people you see and deal with on a daily basis, so the memos, proposals, and reports you send to colleagues and co-workers are often shorter than documents sent outside the company.

Internally, you are also much more likely to share sensitive information that is expected to stay within the walls of your company. So when you write to someone outside your organization, it might be necessary to leave certain information out. Again, I'm not recommending that you ever lie or provide different information to different groups, just that you might change how you phrase things, or not mention them at all if you've been told not to.

For instance, if your company is planning a new product announcement next month, but wants to keep it a secret until then, they won't appreciate it if you mention the product when you send materials to potential customers. You can discuss it with fellow employees all day long, but don't breathe a word of it to people outside the company.

Pro or Con?

Another factor to consider is the attitude or feelings of the people you're writing to. How do they feel about your organization or the issue you're dealing with?

When you're writing to someone, knowing whether they support you or are fighting your efforts is useful. The tone of your letter will be different, as will the way you phrase things. For example, if you're writing a fund raising letter, knowing whether they have donated money in the past may affect what you say to them now. You might mention how grateful your organization was for their previous generous donation.

If the person has never made a donation, you might instead mention why now is such a crucial time for your organization and that you need help from people who've never supported your efforts in the past.

In both cases you're asking for support, but how you ask for it is different.

Level of Familiarity

Whether your audience knows your organization, product, or project also impacts how you address them. The more familiar someone is with your subject, the less background information you need to supply. Chances are, they already know.

However, if your audience consists of a combination of people who know your project inside and out and people who are new to it, you should provide enough background information for those who are new. Err on the side of providing too much information, because without it, part of your audience won't understand what you're talking about.

Tip
Customize the level of detail in your documents depending on how well your audience already knows the topic you're writing about.

What's Their Background?

Once you know who will read your document, you'll want to find out more about them. At the outset you may know who is supposed to read your letter—your boss or the board of directors—but now you need to think about where they're coming from in order to write most effectively. If you write effectively, they will understand your message and see how it affects them.

To write your memo or proposal with the right amount of information, it would be helpful to know some or all of the following:

➤ Are your readers high school or college graduates?

➤ Have they had much technical training?

➤ How much experience do they have in the subject area that you're writing about?

➤ Have they done business with your company before?

➤ Was their experience a positive one?

Knowing more about the experiences that may have shaped your audience's attitude towards the issue you're writing about will help you find the right words to express yourself.

For instance, if you're drafting a sales letter to a current customer, it would be useful to know why this person hasn't done business with you in the last six months. Especially since she had been ordering from you on a regular basis up to that time. Since you're not sure of the reason, but you know that this person has bought from you before, you can start off your letter asking that very question: Did we do something wrong?

Or if you're reporting on the status of your company's new electronic mail system, it would be helpful to know if everyone who is to receive this report knows what the heck electronic mail is. How technical or computer-literate are they? Do they support a new electronic network? With this information in-hand, you can decide whether to write a brief report using the most up-to-date and technical jargon, or whether you should stay low-tech and explain in layman's terms what you mean. You'll be most effective at communicating if you speak to the least technical person's level.

Where Will It Go?

Where will your document be sent after you write it? Since some people are meant to know more than others about situations within your organization, you'll want to know more about where your document is being sent before you finish it.

Within Your Organization or Beyond?

Will your letter, proposal, report, or memo stay within your company or will it be distributed outside the organization as well? That's an important distinction to evaluate as you write.

Depending on whether your document will be circulated internally among your co-workers or externally, among the media, committee members, customers, or suppliers, you may want to add more details or remove some.

You can talk about an important (but secret) project among colleagues, but you certainly wouldn't want to breathe a word of it to someone outside your organization who could alert the competition. You may need to do some editing in that case. But by all means, find out fast who will be reading what you're writing!

For International Use?

Will your materials be used only in your country, or will it be sent to places where English is not the native language? If this is the case, you may want to avoid using colloquial phrases or trendy words that can be misunderstood in other languages. As the business community goes global, making sure your document can be easily translated will become even more essential.

Electronic Distribution

In this age of electronic communication through online systems, you need to determine whether your document will be sent the traditional way—typed on paper—or through cyberspace—using no paper at all.

A consideration with electronic communication is that your message can be forwarded to hundreds or even thousands of other people virtually instantaneously. Your memo can become public within seconds. Just be aware of this and edit your words as needed for your protection.

Electronic communication is one of the least private ways to send information. That doesn't mean you shouldn't use it; just be careful what kind of information you distribute.

When Will They Read It?

In addition to thinking about the situation your readers may be in while they read your document, also think about the time of week or season they may be in.

Is Business Up or Down?

In some businesses, there are clear cycles when sales jump and then drop. For example, retail businesses do a majority of their business between Thanksgiving and Christmas. Landscaping businesses, on the other hand, do much of their work in the spring and fall and are done by the time Thanksgiving rolls around.

So when your proposal for a new advertising campaign lands on the business owner's desk, be aware of whether they have money in their bank account or not. If it's during a slow season, you'll want to emphasize how they can get a jump on the competition, before the big selling time arrives.

Tip
Timing your document to arrive just when a company is open to hearing what you have to say is hard to do. But a little research can improve your chances.

Also take into account the situation your reader is facing at that particular time. For example, if you're sending a letter to a restaurant suggesting that they could benefit from your company's pest control services, it's useful to know if they've had any complaints from customers in the last few months. With that information, you can really customize your message and increase the chance for a positive response. And that's really the point of your writing anyway—to get someone to agree with you, buy your company's services, or improve your own situation in some way.

Tuesday Through Thursday Is Best

The day of the week may also be important. Direct mail studies have shown that Tuesday through Thursday are the best days to have your mail arrive, because the recipient is most likely to open and read it. Monday is bad because there's too much to do after that wild weekend, and by Friday your reader is probably already thinking about going fishing. Either way, chances are good your message won't get read right away.

Why Are You Writing in the First Place?

Is there some particular event or situation that has given you the opportunity to write whatever it is you're writing? For example, has your company decided to lay off a large number of people, causing you to have to prepare letters to management or a press briefing? Has a team of researchers discovered an amazing new cure for stupidity? (Wouldn't that be nice?!)

Sometimes your reason for writing is directly related to who you are writing to. For example, if you are recalling a certain product your company sells, you'd send a letter to all your customers who purchased it. Or if your college is initiating a new campaign, you'd contact the alumni for donations. In each case, the reason for writing and the audience are intertwined.

What this means is that the situation you address can often tell you a lot about your audience and what their reaction may be to your letter or proposal. The situation itself can help in your audience analysis.

How Will They React?

How your audience will potentially react generally depends on whether you're providing good or bad news. Of course, the way you phrase your information will either lessen the blow or make your reader feel even better.

In some cases, the information you're writing about won't be clearly good or bad. Your audience's reaction will be strongly related to whether you think they will support your cause or not. And that question is affected by their relationship to your organization and the issues.

Trying to gauge how your audience will react to your document is tough. But by learning more about their background, you can guess their position. With that information, you can write to garner their continued support or try and sway them your way with your oh-so persuasive arguments.

The Least You Need to Know

➤ Your readers background will affect how he interprets and reacts to your document.

➤ To get your point across effectively, consider your audience's level of responsibility, whether they are part of your organization or not, and their attitudes and familiarity toward the subject you address.

➤ *Where* your document will be read—inside the company or outside, in the U.S. or abroad—is important when choosing your words.

➤ *When* your audience reads your document can impact the response you get from it.

➤ As you write, subtly remind readers why you're writing to them now. Has something significant happened that might affect their situation?

Chapter 5

Creating an Outline to Keep Focused

In This Chapter

➤ How to use an outline to organize your thoughts

➤ Formatting an outline

➤ Filling in the details

➤ "What do I do now?"

Some writers are able to sit down and crank out letters in one fell swoop. They can organize their thoughts fully in their head and feel no need to jot down ideas. The words just go from their minds directly onto the paper almost like magic.

These writers, however, are few and far between. Most people need to write down the facts, ideas, recommendations, and suggestions they want to make before they start composing any kind of document. If you need to think about what you're going to write before you write it, you're in the majority, so don't feel bad.

One tool most writers use to organize their thoughts is an outline. It helps to put each thought or idea into a logical order before getting too far into writing full sentences. The advantage of using an outline is that you can see up front whether the way your information is organized makes sense. Before you start filling in all the details, you know if one thought follows logically from the previous one. Without an outline, you don't really know where you're going to end up. Think of an outline as a road map.

Using an Outline to Stay on Track

It's a good idea to develop an outline before you get too far along in your writing. Doesn't it make sense to figure out what you want to say, what supporting information you want to provide, and how you're going to end your document before you start writing?

You wouldn't get in a car and start driving from New York City to Los Angeles without looking at a map and figuring out which roads to travel, would you? So don't start writing before you map out all the important twists and turns you want to take in your writing.

Some people research their writing topic first, instead of creating an outline. They gather books and articles and conduct interviews, depending on the type of project they're involved in. Maybe you've done this before, too.

The problem with this approach is that you'll probably end up researching a lot of information that really isn't relevant. You'll waste time and energy going in directions that won't be useful. You'll have note cards and pieces of paper with notes on them that you'll end up throwing away later.

Instead, create your outline before you start researching. Yes, if you don't know much about the topic at hand, your outline will be very general, but at least you can write down the questions you want to answer. This way, as you scan different sources or talk with people to gather ideas, you can immediately decide whether that information is important or not to your assignment. If it answers a question you've posed in your outline, you'll probably want to write it down. But if it doesn't fit with any of your key questions, you probably don't need it.

Determining If It Fits

Each question or major topic in your outline is called a *heading*. Your heading summarizes the information that's going to be covered in the next section of your outline and your paper.

As you take notes or write down ideas, try to determine where the information fits in your outline. Next, somewhere on your note card or next to the note on your piece of paper, scribble the title of the section heading from your outline where you think it belongs. This doesn't mean you can't change your mind later or move it around somewhere else. It's just an initial check to make sure that the information you collect has a general place to go within your outline.

Later, as you skim your notes and fill in your outline, you can quickly put all your thoughts in place according to the section title you wrote down. Pile all your notes for the first section in one place and all the notes for the second section somewhere else, and so on. This helps you organize your information much faster.

If you can't find an appropriate section where you think the information will fit, it probably doesn't belong in your outline at all. Don't even bother writing it down.

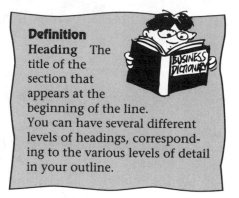

Definition
Heading   The title of the section that appears at the beginning of the line. You can have several different levels of headings, corresponding to the various levels of detail in your outline.

What Does an Outline Look Like?

An outline is fairly easy to put together—it's not complex or involved, just very orderly. The information in an outline flows from general to specific. The broadest categories appear first and are followed by more specific pieces of supporting information.

So that you can tell how all the information is related, there is a format for setting up an outline. Each piece of information is put on its own line on a piece of paper so that they don't all run together. It's also easier to move them around. Major categories of information, like the chapters of a book, are put on their own lines, left justified, with a capital letter in front of them. These are headings. Outlines use letters and numbers to help keep information orderly.

Capital letters are for the largest and most general categories. Numbers are for the next biggest categories and small letters are for even more specific categories and pieces of information. Depending on how detailed you want to get with your outline, you can also continue to build on it using alternating numbers and letters. But the format is always letters followed by numbers followed by letters, and so on.

Tip
Letters and numbers used in an outline always appear in the proper alphabetical or numeric order. You'd never see an "A" heading followed by a "3," followed by a "c." It's always capital letter, followed by number 1, followed by either number 2 and so on, or lowercase a.

In addition to switching back and forth from letters to numbers to letters, each time you get more specific with your information, you indent the line. This helps your eye see how the information is related.

This is how a basic blank outline should look.

A.

    1.

        a.

           1)

Generally, you'll have more than one subject under each heading. So after the "1," you probably need to have a "2," "3," and "4," depending on how long your document is. The point is, as long as you use this format, you can have many different level headings. Here is a sample of what a more involved blank outline might look like:

A.

    1.

    2.

        a.

        b.

        c.

    3.

        a.

        b.

           1)

           2)

B.

    1.

        a.

        b.

    2.

        a.

        b.

Of course, after each letter or number, you would have a short phrase to summarize the point that you want to make. Don't write in complete sentences because you'll waste too much time. Short phrases are fine for now. Once your outline is complete you can go back in and fill in more detail.

Generally you won't need to get much more detailed than the fourth level, where your subheadings start with a 1), 2), and so on.

Of course, you're creating an outline now based on limited knowledge, which means that your outline is probably going to change quite a bit once you've learned something about your topic.

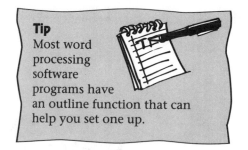

Tip
Most word processing software programs have an outline function that can help you set one up.

If you're familiar with what you're writing about, your outline will be pretty complete from the start. Your research or information gathering will simply help fill in some details. But you may not need to move things around much.

How Do You Use One?

First, write down every topic you want to touch on in your letter, memo, proposal, report, note, press release—whatever. Don't worry about the order in which they come to you, just write them down on a piece of paper, or type them into your computer. Some people like note cards; use one note card per idea to make them easier to organize later.

Sometimes it's easiest to write general questions that you know you'll need to answer in your report. Other times, short phrases are good, such as when you type up a proposal to a client and you know what areas you have to talk about.

After you're satisfied that you've identified all the important issues or topics, you can start fitting them into the rough outline. Take each idea or note one at a time and refer back to your outline to determine where that idea should be placed. Write it down under a numbered heading. Then go to the next idea and write it where it fits best, until you've gone through your entire list of topics.

Obviously, with some assignments you'll have a gazillion items to write about, such as when you're putting together a multimillion-dollar bid or proposal. More often you'll only have four or five subjects to tackle.

Here's a sample outline for a new product press release, to show you what a finished one would look like:

THE NEW IMPROVED KITCHEN SINK

A. Product description

    1. What it looks like

    2. How it works

    3. What's new about it

B. Advantages over competitors' products

    1. Size

        a. Holds more dishes

    2. Appearance

        a. Comes in 100 different colors

        b. Can be customized for any kitchen

    3. Features

        a. Garbage disposal can chop any hard material

        b. Self-cleaning

        c. Faucet turns on and off automatically

    4. Price

        a. Less expensive

        b. Can be financed

C. How to order

    1. When it will be available

    2. Phone number to call for local dealers

    3. Internet address

Where Do You Go Once It's Written?

Unfortunately, a well-developed outline is not an end to your writing; it's just a beginning. Yes, you're done organizing your material, but now you actually have to start writing.

It's time to flesh out the ideas from your outline. One way to do that is to take the topic described on your heading line as your first sentence. Then follow that sentence with more detail regarding what you've just said. Generally, you'll cover that extra detail in the next heading below it. If not, move on to the next topic or add some additional information on your own, not found in the outline.

Sometimes you'll need to add transitional sentences to make your language flow smoothly from topic to topic. You may also think of other points to make as you write. That's fine. Just write them down.

When your first draft is complete, set it aside overnight if you have time. Then reread it in the morning to see where it sounds choppy. Those are the areas where you need more transitional phrases or more detail.

Don't rely on your outline to write every sentence of your document. It's only meant to be a guide to the major topics you want to write about. It shouldn't be so detailed that you can write a sentence for each subheading—if you can, you spent too much time developing your outline. But don't worry about it now, just keep it in mind for your next letter or article.

> **Tip**
> Transitional phrases and sentences are those that link two different thoughts with words such as "and," "nonetheless," "consequently," and "however."

The Least You Need to Know

➤ The first step in creating an outline is writing down every topic you want to talk about in your document.

➤ After you identify all the subjects to be addressed, you can then prioritize them, or put them into the order in which you'll write about them.

➤ Each line of an outline is preceded by a letter or number, depending on how specific the piece of information is.

➤ Once you have a framework to guide you, start gathering information to use in your proposal, report, memo or letter to fill in the details.

Chapter 6

Generating Initial Ideas

In This Chapter

➤ How to get started

➤ What to write when you can't begin

➤ When editing is counterproductive

➤ Expanding sentence fragments into a complete project

People who have a hard time with writing often procrastinate. And it's understandable; we all have those activities we really don't want to do. You know, those tasks we recognize are going to be a challenge.

Fortunately, writing doesn't have to be one of those gut-wrenching efforts. The more you do it, the more you realize that it's fairly easy. Becoming more comfortable with the process of writing can help you view it as just another job that needs to be done, rather than a chore to be avoided. And the only way to become comfortable with something is to practice.

Think about Olympic athletes who perform amazing feats with apparent ease. Of course, we never saw the years of practice that went into that gravity-defying jump or record-breaking swimming pace. It's the same with writing. The more you work on your skill, the better you'll get and the simpler it will seem. The key is mustering the courage to put those first words down on paper, whether you're writing with a pen or pencil or typing on a computer keyboard or typewriter.

Getting Started Is the Toughest Part

Seeing a blank piece of paper is daunting. You worry about how you're going to fill that open space with words. It seems like an awful lot of space. You wonder whether you really have that much to say. Well, stop worrying.

Warning
The longer your document is, the less likely it is that someone will actually read it to the end. So keep it short.

Don't concern yourself with how many words or pages you need to fill. That's really not important. Length or quantity isn't what counts; it's quality and clarity that you should be shooting for.

Besides, the more you worry, the less you want to start writing. Don't make the project out to be harder than it really is. Stop telling yourself how difficult it will be and how much time it will take. Once you begin, you'll be amazed at how quickly you can make serious progress.

Tip
Writing about why you can't start writing is another approach. You may discover what's holding you back, or at least, get some words on the page.

Chapter 9, "Breaking Through Writer's Block," has some tips for jump-starting your thinking if you get stuck. And there are plenty of us who get to a certain point and can't go any further.

Getting stuck *before* you begin is a special kind of writer's block related to anxiety. Many people are afraid to get started on their project because they fear what will happen when they finish.

Don't Think Ahead

It may sound crazy, but imagine if your assignment is to write a memo informing your staff that you need to lay off half of them. You're probably going to dread writing the memo because of the aftermath.

You wonder how your employees will take the news; how they'll react. You try and come up with the nicest way possible to break the news to them so that it will hurt the least. And part of you thinks that if you didn't ever get around to writing the memo, maybe you wouldn't have to go through with the job cuts.

The truth is, the job cuts will occur whether you finish the memo or not. And you'll be in less hot water with your boss if you just finish the darned thing ASAP!

Stop worrying about the events that your memo will bring about and just focus on the task itself—writing the memo. If you think about "what comes next," your mind will wander and you'll never get it done.

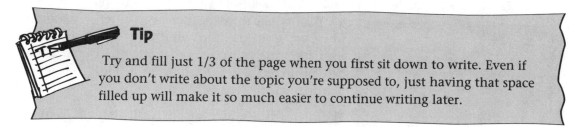

Tip

Try and fill just 1/3 of the page when you first sit down to write. Even if you don't write about the topic you're supposed to, just having that space filled up will make it so much easier to continue writing later.

Write Down Any Idea That Comes to You

One trick that writers use to get them started on a writing project is just to start writing anything. And I mean literally, anything.

Write a Letter to Mom

You might start with a letter to your mother, just to ease yourself into the practice of writing without bringing on the tension associated with your current project. Tell her about what's going on at work, or if that's too boring for mom, describe how your kids are doing at school, or the renovations you've just completed on your house.

Write About Things You Enjoy

Another suggestion is to start by writing down what you did last weekend that was fun; sort of like those "what I did last summer" reports from grade school. Keep it fun and simple. Writing this helps to reassure yourself that your other project will be just as easy to write.

Build Your Confidence

Part of the reason for writing about something familiar to you is that you feel more confident. The more you know about something, the easier it is to write about. You don't stumble over words or struggle to figure out what you want to say.

The same is true about public speaking. People fear speaking in public and making presentations more than they fear death. And the biggest part of the

Quote

Learn more than you need to know to write the story, until you totally understand the situation. Then you can boil it down and explain it.

Linda Stern, a regular contributor to *Newsweek* and a syndicated personal finance columnist.

problem is that they don't feel confident. They aren't convinced that they know their subject inside and out.

So the solution, obviously, is to research and practice what you're going to say about your topic. This helps you feel confident of your abilities to answer any question that comes up. With public speaking, you need to get to a point where you feel almost certain that you know more about the subject than anyone in the audience. The trick in becoming comfortable speaking in public is to practice, practice, practice.

Tip

When you tire of writing about other topics, start to put down some thoughts related to your project. You can do it gradually, such as in your letter to mom, or you can switch directly to your memo—whatever your mind is comfortable doing.

The same is true for writing, in many respects. Even for the shortest memo or letter, you need to feel confident that you understand why you're writing, who you're writing to, and what may happen as a result. Once you know that, you're home free, which is where practice comes in. You need to write about something you're familiar with, just to build your confidence.

Sentence Fragments Are OK

You don't have to spend an exorbitant amount of time writing in complete sentences. At first, ideas and notes are fine. Initially you're just building your confidence by listing everything you need to mention in your letter, memo, or article. Put together an outline to help you organize your ideas (see Chapter 5 for a refresher).

Once you have all your ideas down, go back and put your ideas in order, and fill in the details to make your writing sound smooth.

No Editing Allowed

Editing and polishing the first draft of your document is crucial. Don't ever think you can get away without some level of editing. Set aside time after getting all your thoughts down on paper to review and reflect on what you've written.

Did you write about everything you wanted to or is something still missing? Do all your thoughts flow from one to the next easily and logically? Is everything spelled correctly? These are all things you'll need to think about when you start editing.

BUT NOT NOW!

Let me repeat: Editing is a big part of writing, but it isn't done until later.

Creating a first draft and editing are two totally separate parts of writing. Don't mix them together. If you do, you'll just slow down the process of getting your thoughts on paper. We'll get into editing later, after you've learned a little more about some of the basics of writing.

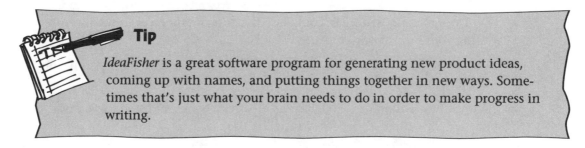

Tip

Brainstorming involves getting several people together to generate ideas. Participants call out suggestions and thoughts that are then written down. No one evaluates or comments on any of the ideas until everyone is done coming up with new thoughts. When you're writing, try and follow the same guidelines—don't evaluate or throw out any idea at first.

Where to Go for Inspiration

If you just can't seem to make any headway on your own, turn to some tools that may jumpstart your thinking.

Products

There are creativity products, from books to card decks, that pose questions to help you see different approaches to situations. They are helpful in that they expand your thought processes. However, these types of items are probably good to use when you aren't facing a deadline for your writing project.

Tip

IdeaFisher is a great software program for generating new product ideas, coming up with names, and putting things together in new ways. Sometimes that's just what your brain needs to do in order to make progress in writing.

Relaxation Techniques

Another way to get your mind going is to get away from your writing altogether. That means take a half hour walk, get some exercise at the gym, go for a scenic drive, or try some other relaxing activity to help your mind wander. Changing your surroundings can trigger new ideas and help you come up with a list of things to say in your document.

Turn to Your Advisors

In some cases, you may need to discuss your project with someone else. It helps to talk things over with co-workers or colleagues whom you trust. A friend of mine has a business advisor she calls monthly to talk over situations that crop up. You should look for people whom you can turn to for feedback and brainstorming.

I have a group of fellow business owners I can call when faced with a writing task that I'm just not comfortable with. I explain the situation, tell them how I'm planning to approach it, or read what I've already written, and ask for suggestions on what they would do.

From them, I get new ideas that help improve my writing, as well as reassurance and encouragement that I'm on the right track. In most cases, that's all I really needed anyway and the suggestions are an added bonus.

Sleep on It

Some professionals who are trying to do too much find that rest is what is needed to get their brain back in gear. Crawling into bed early may be just what you need to help your brain rest so you can sort out your thoughts in the morning.

Of course, I sometimes find myself relying on sleep as a way to procrastinate. So unless you know you're really tired, I'd suggest sticking with writing until you have at least 1/3 of the page filled with words.

The Least You Need to Know

➤ Get into the swing of writing by drafting a letter or scribbling some random thoughts.

➤ Don't worry about writing in complete thoughts or sentences. Just concentrate on getting your ideas down on paper.

➤ Hold off on editing anything you've written. Once you start editing, you stop generating new ideas.

➤ Taking a break, flipping through some creativity books, or listening to music can help get your mind in gear for writing.

Writing a First Draft

Writing a first draft is no big deal. Those of you who are afraid of tackling your writing project head-on need to understand what a first draft is and isn't. You shouldn't dread starting to write one, or be concerned that it won't be good enough. First drafts aren't meant to be the final version of anything, just the first try.

Perfectionists have a really hard time with first drafts. Do you know why? Because they don't understand what a "draft" is. They think that when they start writing they only have one chance to get everything into place. Truthfully, unless you're working within an extremely tight deadline, you should have plenty of time to go back and rewrite anything in your draft you don't like. So relax.

Using Your Outline as a Guide

A draft of something is a first attempt, a trial run, a sort of test. It involves combining your ideas and notes with the outline you've created. Does this sound complicated? It really isn't. You're simply putting all the pieces together to make a written document.

Since you've written an outline for your project, you've already decided what you wanted to talk about in your report, memo, article, and so on. Even if your outline is based on questions you need to answer, rather than specific points you have to address, at least you know a little bit about what you're going to say. Now you just need to start answering the questions in your outline based on any information gathering you've done.

Taking Notes

Sometimes when you start to write something, you'll realize that you don't need to do any research or information gathering at all. You know what you want to say and you don't need any additional information at all.

This might be the case if, for example, you were writing a warning letter to an employee who is always late for work. Since you know the employee's name, that he frequently arrives 15 minutes late, and that it causes problems for other employees who have to rely on him, you're all set.

However, to be sure you have a complete picture of the situation, you could do a little fact checking if you wanted. You could start by checking the employee's personnel file to see if any other supervisors ever reported him being late or if there have been other written warnings for any reason. If you find the employee is on probation, you may have to change the wording of your letter to be a bit more stern or threatening.

In every situation, you'll probably find that you have to talk to someone or look in a file in order to double-check some information you have. Whenever you're trying to find a particular piece of information or do a little investigating about something, you're going to want to make note of it. That means you're going to want to write it down.

> **Tip**
>
> You may have the best memory in the world, but it really helps to have something in writing in case you have to turn over the project to someone else later on. It also increases the chances of reporting accurate information. We tend to forget a lot, but writing something down right away improves the odds that it will get reported correctly. And if the information is ever questioned later, you have proof of what you discovered in writing.

What Your Notes Should Contain

Unlike Mr. Spock, we humans haven't figured out how to do a mind meld to transfer information from one person to another. Old fashioned notes are still the way to go. When you take notes, the key pieces of information you need are:

➤ Who said it, wrote it, or reported it

➤ What did they say

➤ When did they say it

If you can fit in other details that you think are relevant, feel free. For example, if you're writing an article on your company's new drug that helps cancer victims fight the disease, you'll probably want to find out some statistics on cancer survival rates, what kinds of procedures are used, and what percent of cancer patients can be helped by your company's product. It's unlikely that you'll just intuitively know these facts off the top of your head. Most people would need to turn to recent medical journals or articles to learn more about cancer survival rates.

When taking notes from facts you find in articles, books, and reports, you'd want to note whatever the important information was, the name of the article and magazine where it appeared, and the issue that it was in. The name of the author and the page number on which it appeared is also good to write down.

Quote
The City Editor's mantra: Write it right, write it tight, and write it tonight!

Provided by **Todd Garber** of Enid, Oklahoma.

Tip
The Encyclopedia of Associations can give you the names and phone numbers of any association or society in the world. These types of groups often collect statistics that may be helpful in your information gathering. Most public libraries have a copy you can use for free.

This helps in a couple of different ways. First, when you report information from an outside source, you need to give credit where credit is due. If you don't, that's called plagiarism. It's illegal. Whenever you use someone else's idea, thought, or words, you need to let everyone know. You can't pretend that you came up with it on your own.

It's also to your benefit to report information from another source; it gives you credibility and believability. For instance, if you were to say that you believed cholesterol is good for us, people would be less likely to believe you than if you said that the National Institute of Health found that cholesterol is good. People may not know you, but they've probably heard of the National Institute of Health and know that they're a legitimate research organization.

Secondly, if you ever need to refer back to the article that you read or the book you took out, you'll have all the details you need to track it down again.

Notecards Are Lifesavers

When you start writing down your notes and ideas, it helps to put them in one place. Having notes in several places, in a few different formats can become confusing. You're also likely to lose information, or at least misplace it.

The solution is to pick one way to take notes and stick with it. It'll make your life easier. It doesn't really matter how you record your notes, but keeping them together will make a difference.

Cards, notebooks, and file folders are three of the most popular ways to keep notes organized and together. And you can use them in conjunction with one another if you find that it's easier.

Notecards

Three by five index cards are popular tools for taking notes. You can write down a single idea or point on one card and then file it away in a small box or in a file folder for safe keeping.

The advantage is that you're limited to one idea per card. You also can't go overboard in how much you write because there is only so much space.

One way to divide up the space on the card is to note the person's name who was speaking, or the author of an important book, in the top left-hand corner of the card. Then write the name of the article, book, report, or conference where you found the information directly beneath the person's name. Page numbers are a good idea, too.

Tip

Try to write as neatly as possible when taking notes. It can take more time to figure out what you meant than it would if you just write carefully.

In the lined section of the card, you can write down the point that you want to remember, or the statistic that is important.

Then in the upper right-hand corner you can note the section of your outline that the information fits in. This will really make things easier later when you can shuffle through your cards and create a pile for each section of your outline.

Notebook

A spiral or three-ring notebook is another approach to taking notes and keeping them together. The advantage is that you don't have to deal with lots of individual cards.

But the disadvantage is that you'll have a laundry list of notes to contend with when you're done.

If you choose a notebook for notetaking, you may want to put the author's information at the top of the page to help you keep track of who said what. And then write on the front and back of the page, if necessary, what the person said. Start a new page for each new source.

File Folder

Manila or hanging file folders are useful when you're collecting information from several different sources.

I have file folders for lots of ongoing projects. When I come across something related to a project, I just throw it in the folder. Ideas written on scraps of paper, notes, articles, letters, and memos all go in there. Then when I need to write something up, I already have most of my research done and in one place.

Tip
Whether you decide to write down your ideas on cards, lined paper, or scrap notepads, it's a good idea to place everything in a central folder.

Fitting Your Ideas into Your Outline

Your outline can help you sort out what information is useful to write down and what information isn't.

Your Notetaking Guide

Use your outline to help you choose whether a particular piece of information is relevant. Essentially, if you can't find a section in your outline where a certain fact or statement would fit, you can throw it out. Or at least, don't bother writing it down.

It's easiest to start at the top of your outline, taking a look at the first topic in your "A" heading. Now write down all your ideas and thoughts related to that topic. If you're using notecards, remember to put only one piece of information on each card. Jot down the section title in the upper right-hand corner of the card.

After you've scanned all your background material, looking for information that would fit in your "A" section, move on to the next topic area and go through the same process.

When you're finished with your materials, you'll end up with a complete outline and several pieces of information that will form your first draft.

Sorting Out the Garbage

Another way that your outline helps you immensely is that it saves you time by sorting out all of the irrelevant information. For example, if you're in search of information on employee incentive programs for a proposal you're putting together, your outline will help weed out stuff you don't need to bother with. For example, that article on advertising specialties doesn't appear to fit anywhere in your outline. SO DON'T READ IT.

And if you insist on reading it to be sure that you don't miss a brilliant idea, don't take any notes unless you find a section in your outline that the information would fit in.

Prioritizing Helps

Armed with your notes and your outline, you're now ready to begin writing. At last!

Start with your "A" heading in your outline, just as you did with your notetaking. Now pull out all the notecards or slips of paper with information that fits that section. Read through them so that you're more familiar with the information.

Sifting Through Your Notes

Think about each tidbit of information and decide which note to write about first. Your first point should be your highest priority, your most relevant or interesting point. Your next point should be the second most vital statement. And so on.

Don't start writing yet, just rearrange all your cards or notes into an order according to their level of priority. Your "1" and "2" level headings from your outline can also be a guide to which point to write about first, second, third, and so on.

Combining Them to Form a Draft

Once your cards are all in order, you're ready to write. Take a look again at the issue you're supposed to address first—your "A" heading in your outline—and pick up the first card, featuring information about the most important point you want to make. Think about how they relate, how they go together.

> **Quote**
>
> Write down a sentence summarizing each important point you want to make. Then go back and write another sentence expanding on that first one, then another expanding on your second until you've provided enough detail to make your point.
>
> **Charles Turner**, General Manager, Cricket on the Hearth in Penfield, New York.

Now write a sentence stating what your note has to do with your topic. That wasn't so bad, was it?

Put that first card in a pile and pick up the second notecard. Go through the same process. Think about how it relates to your topic and write a sentence about it. If you need to write more than one sentence to complete the thought, then feel free to write away. You're really gaining momentum now.

Just keep going through your notes, following the order you've set in your outline, and write one or two sentences for every note you've taken.

Filling in the Missing Pieces

After you've gone through all your cards, you have the makings of a first draft. All your ideas are down on paper, you just need to polish it up a bit.

Read through your first and second sentences. Do they flow smoothly from one to the next? Probably not. How can you elaborate on your first point to make it connect to the second? What kind of transition phrases or sentences can you add that would show how the two sentences have something in common?

Go through your draft and fill in a sentence here and there to make it less choppy. You'll probably want to read through it a few times to see where else you need to add sentences. And when you reach a point that you can't see where else you can add anything, you have a first draft. Voilà!

Quote
Go back and add detail. Picture a box of crayolas—the big one with the sharpener. Don't just say red, say vermillion, or brick, or rose.

Linda Stern, *Newsweek* contributor and a syndicated personal finance columnist.

The Least You Need to Know

➤ Think of your first draft as a first attempt and don't get hung up on trying to make it sound perfect.

➤ When taking notes, write down who said it, what they said, and where it appeared.

➤ File everything related to a writing project in a central file folder.

➤ Match the subject of each notecard with a section of your outline in order to begin writing your draft.

➤ When doing any information gathering, don't waste time on topics that aren't directly related to your document. Think of the sections of your outline as your priorities and don't stray from them.

"YOU KEEP SPELLING "CANTALOUPE" WRONG.

Chapter 8

Editing and Polishing

In This Chapter

➤ Checking for completeness

➤ Editing basics

➤ Professional proofreading how tos

➤ The role of an editor

Once you've reached the stage of actually having a first draft, pat yourself on the back. You're almost home-free. Getting all your ideas down on paper, in an order that makes sense, is an accomplishment.

Now all you need to do is tidy it up a bit. Don't be tempted by the thought of sending out your draft as it is. Yes, all your ideas are in print. Yes, you've probably made all the important points. And yes, you can still improve on them.

Definition
Typographical Errors
Mistakes that are made in using a typewriter or keyboard to type up a document. When your fingers hit an "s" instead of an "a," that's a typographical error. However, when you misspell the word "computer," that's not typographical—it's just incorrect.

If you send out your letter, memo, report or whatever without at least reviewing it a second time (at a minimum), you risk being caught with typos, choppy sentences, and incomplete thoughts. It's much smarter to let your draft sit overnight, so you can read it again in the morning when your mind is fresh. Your eyes are also better able to catch glaring errors that your computer missed.

The process of editing really involves improving on your first draft. You want to check that your work is complete and that you've addressed all the important issues. You also want to look out for errors—grammatical, spelling, and typographical—by proofreading the whole document.

Have You Said Everything You Wanted to Say?

When you get to the editing stage, you're really getting one last chance to add information that should be there. As you read your document again, consider whether you've raised any new questions that haven't been answered. If you find that you have, you'll need to go back and add some details.

Quote
It's been my experience that most non-pro writers write something once and only once; twice at the most. With rare exception, I constantly re-edit and rewrite my stuff until I can hear it singing.

The writing muscle is like any other. It needs to be exercised and used to stay toned.

Elaine Petrowski, freelance writer in Ridgewood, New Jersey who has been published in *The New York Times*, *House Beautiful*, and *Home Mechanix*, to name a few.

For example, let's say you're sending a complaint letter to a vendor because the forms that he printed a few months ago were on the wrong paper. In your letter you've pointed out that you provided the artwork and specifications that he should have followed, but apparently didn't. You've reviewed the sequence of events to familiarize the president of the company with what occurred. And you've thanked him for his time.

Sound like an OK letter to you? It sounds pretty good to me except that I'm left wondering why you bothered to write it in the first place. What's the purpose? Did you just need to vent your frustration or place the blame squarely on someone else's shoulders? *Or* did you also mean to ask for the job to be reprinted at no cost? Or perhaps you want a refund of what you've already paid because you had to go to another printer to have it produced correctly? Or, because of the long-standing relationship between your two companies, did you just want to make the owner aware of how displeased you are?

Whatever the reason, you need to state it. Otherwise, you leave the owner bewildered as to what he's supposed to do to cheer you up. Make it easy on him—tell him exactly what you want. In other instances, you may review your letter and discover that those paragraphs toward the end really aren't necessary. You've made your point and you don't need to belabor it. So cut those extra sentences.

Try to read your letter from your recipient's point of view. And then add or subtract information to make it as easy as possible for the person to understand why you're writing and what you want him or her to do about it.

What Did You Miss?

The role of an editor is to help you identify those missing links and to suggest new ways of making your point. Most of us don't have access to an editor for our everyday memos and letters, but we can rely on co-workers and colleagues to give us valuable second opinions.

Or if that's not possible, you can serve as your own editor. The disadvantage is that sometimes you may get too close to your own writing to be able to judge it effectively. Just keep that in mind and look for opportunities to get an outside opinion.

Content Editing

One level of editing involves reviewing the content, or factual information in your document. You'll want to double-check that the statistics you've stated are accurate and that the description of a certain procedure is right.

You don't have to call in the experts to do this—just review your notes if anything doesn't sound right. Compare what you noted to what you ended up writing in your report. Are they the same? If they are, then you're OK. If you've slanted the meaning a bit, you'll want to rewrite it.

Technical Editing

Another level of editing involves more of the technical aspects of writing; those involving grammar, spelling, and punctuation.

Once you've confirmed that your information is correct, you need to be sure you've spelled it correctly, too. You'll also want to read through your sentences to check whether they're grammatically correct. We'll get into more grammar basics in the next chapter.

> **Quote**
> Once you've proofed your writing for the last time, go through it once more. Print out a clean copy of your material, sit down in a quiet place where you'll encounter few distractions, and proof it for inconsistencies. For example, are the company names spelled and capitalized the same way throughout?
>
> **Mary Anne Brugnoni,** Brugnoni Design of Pittsford, New York.

Proofreading Tips

Proofreading is another way of saying "looking for mistakes." A proofreader's job is to carefully look over written documents to identify and correct any spelling errors, grammatical goofs, and typos (short for typographical errors).

Quote
When someone else is going to edit your writing, type in a double-spaced format so he or she has room to write changes or comments.

Sandra Beckwith, Editor and publisher, *The Do(o)little Report.*

Spelling errors are probably the easiest to spot. With today's technology, a lot of first round proofreading can be done by computer. Programs within word-processing software can now find misspelled words, grammatically questionable phrases, and repeated words. But don't rely on your spell-checker program as your only proofreading tool. It's a good start, but the problem is that you can have a correctly spelled word in a spot where you meant to have a different word entirely. For instance, "and" where you meant to have "an" is a common occurrence. Or "the" when you intended to say "then." Both words are spelled right, so your spell checker would let it go. Unless you read through your document manually, using your own eyes, that mistake would go undetected.

Once you have a draft that you feel confident is almost ready to distribute, read through your document again in search of errors. There are common proofreading symbols used to explain what is wrong with what is on the page (see the following table). These are particularly useful if someone else, such as an assistant or editor, is going to be typing the changes. The notations are a way of communicating what you want fixed.

Tip
Reading sentences backward is a proofreading trick. It forces you to focus on the spelling of each word and makes you more accurate.

It's wise to have others read through your document as well, even if they don't have formal proofreading experience. The reason we often don't catch even some of the most obvious mistakes is that our eyes subconsciously see what we expect to be on the page. If you meant to type "the new table is manufactured of mahogany" you expect it to be spelled that way. Your eyes imagine that this is what's on the page. However, someone who hasn't ever read your document, such as a new purchaser, is going to see that, in fact, mahogany is typed "mahogeny" on the page. You've become so familiar with what should be on the page that you can't see what's actually there. So run your memos and letters by someone else just in case.

Proofreaders use standard symbols to indicate what needs to be done to correct a word or sentence.

The Least You Need to Know

➤ Editing involves improving on your first draft by identifying mistakes that are there and pieces of missing information that aren't.

➤ When editing your document, verify the content of your message as well as check the way you've written it.

➤ Computer programs can find simple errors, but don't rely on them entirely for your proofreading.

➤ Reading your writing backward, from start to finish, helps you see incorrectly spelled words.

Chapter 9

Breaking Through Writer's Block

At one point or another virtually everyone has experienced writer's block. If you've ever found yourself staring at a blank page unable to come up with anything to say, you've been "blocked." Whether you're a college student, business owner, or professional writer, if you have a project that involves writing, you're a candidate for writer's block. Even Mark Twain suffered from writer's block.

Writer's block is extremely common and can wreak havoc on your productivity and efficiency. Of course, it generally appears at the most inconvenient times, like when you're struggling to finish up that important multi-million dollar proposal or overdue report.

To get beyond writer's block, you need to recognize when you're experiencing it, take steps to get around it, and finish up the project at hand. I'm going to give you some tips and suggestions to help you on both counts. So when it's 10 p.m. and you're still at the office and just can't seem to find the words to finish that memo, you can try a new strategy for breaking writer's block that will get your writing done faster.

What Does Writer's Block Feel Like?

Remember Jack Nicholson's character in the movie "The Shining?" In the movie he moves himself and his family into an isolated (and deserted) mountain resort with the intention of finishing his first novel. At first the solitude seems to be just what the novelist needs, but by the end of the story, it has become clear that he's not making especially good progress. The murderous climax occurs when his wife discovers that his "novel" consists of nothing but pages and pages of the simple phrase, "All work and no play makes Jack a dull boy." When Jack discovers that he's been found out, all hell breaks loose.

Definition
Writer's Block An inability to get started, or to continue, with the process of working on a written project, such as an article, memo, letter, or proposal. It is the feeling of not being able to find the words to express whatever it is that needs to be expressed. If you don't address the situation, you can waste considerable time and cause yourself unneeded stress.

While writer's block doesn't generally have such catastrophic results, most of us have experienced the profound frustration of reaching for words that just won't come. Writers aren't the only creative types who experience blockages—it happens from time to time to artists, musicians, indeed nearly everyone.

The encouraging thing is that the feeling of being stuck doesn't last forever. Some people experience writer's block before starting any writing assignment or activity; and most of us have no idea how to stop the cycle. The strategies in this chapter will help you avoid writer's block altogether, or to break through it if you do find that you're stuck.

What Causes It?

Generally, when you set expectations of yourself that are beyond your comfort level, or put undue pressure on yourself to perform, writer's block can set in.

There are many reasons you may find it difficult to start writing. Do any of the following sound familiar to you?

Believing that whatever you put down on paper has to be perfect the first time through.

Thinking that you can't write as well as you'd like to, so what's the point?

Being concerned about what others will think when they read what you've written.

Fear of success and the responsibilities that it will bring.

Focusing on the potential overwhelming results of the writing project you're working on, rather than the project itself (try not to think about the huge impact your report will have on your company, just write).

Fear of failure, or focusing on what may happen to you if you don't get this thing written.

Thinking that the exercise is futile—that it won't really matter in the long run, so why even do it?

Convincing yourself that there are other things you need to do before you get started on this (some may seem important and others may be trivial and distracting).

While we've probably all had similar thoughts at one time or another, you need to try to stay focused on the task in front of you, rather than getting all worked up over trying to be perfect (believe me it won't be, nor does it have to be, perfect). You also need to avoid becoming distracted by other tasks that won't help get the writing done.

Some people get so carried away by other things that need to be done that they simply can't start writing until they've taken care of everything else first. You know, the sudden urge to mop the kitchen floor or scrub the fingerprints off the refrigerator door. While these things probably need to be taken care of at some point, they don't have to be dealt with until after you've written something. So tell yourself that as you fight the inclination to do some heavy-duty cleaning.

Quote
The Oliver Stone formula for successful writing: butt to chair.

Barbara Tone

Try to be aware of what's going through your mind as you struggle to get it in gear. Whatever thoughts and fears are there are probably a good indication of why you haven't put pen to paper yet.

Types of Writer's Block

There are six major types of block, according to Jerrold Mundis, author of *Break Writer's Block Now!* and many other books and articles. (Obviously, he's managed to work through his writer's block.) I know which form causes me the most grief—which one is your personal demon?

Full Paralysis

When you absolutely can't make any headway on a writing project, no matter how hard you try, you're probably experiencing full paralysis. Nothing is coming to mind, you can't think of anything useful, and the words are nonexistent.

Avoidance Behavior

Yup, this is the one I've perfected. When I absolutely must sit down and finish up that cover letter to a client, I can always think of something else that needs to be done first, such as cleaning off my desk. Suddenly a clean, well-organized desktop becomes my highest priority. I bunch all my papers into little piles and then begin filing them in my filing cabinet when I notice that I really should have new hanging folders. So I run to the office supply store to pick some up.

On my return I notice that there are a lot of client files that really need to be weeded out, so I start that project. I move old files to storage boxes that I then carry to the storage room. By the end of the afternoon, my desk is clear, my filing cabinet actually has space in it for new files, but my cover letter is no closer to being done than it was four hours ago. Instead of feeling like I've accomplished a lot, I'm more stressed because I haven't made any progress on my writing.

This is avoidance at its best.

I never really thought about it as avoidance behavior; I just thought I was getting distracted. But the truth is that I wanted to be distracted—anything to keep me from getting bogged down with work. Do you find yourself also becoming distracted? Then perhaps you're also trying to avoid beginning to write.

Last-Minute Crisis Writing

Some of us believe that we work best under pressure. You know, if you leave something to the last minute, it forces you to concentrate and really produce something insightful. (I've said that so many times to people). But it's a good excuse for procrastination, isn't it?

When you put off writing a document until just before you have to present it to your boss, to a committee, or to a client, you're putting unnecessary pressure on yourself. Instead of determining how to express something, you become more worried about the minutes ticking away on the clock. This causes you stress and lessens your concentration.

Inability to Select Between Projects

Do you often find yourself having trouble deciding which project to tackle first, because they are all important and all overdue? Instead of sitting down, choosing a document and starting, you spend a huge amount of time trying to prioritize your work. You put off writing by becoming mired in the process of selection.

Inability to Finish a Piece

While many people find getting started the hardest part, others just can't seem to finish. You may have written a draft, or maybe just a section, but you can't seem to sit down and put the finishing touches on the project. You may feel like you just can't face that project again. So you don't. And it doesn't get done. You're blocked.

Block Specific

Ever have days when you're incredibly productive? You finish up some projects, clean and organize your desk, and return all your important phone calls. But you still haven't made any headway on that one writing project that really needs to be done. This is "block specific" writer's block. It doesn't matter whether the project is big or small, you just can't force yourself to work on it. But you can still work on just about anything else.

How to Combat It

Just as there are lots of reasons you get writer's block, there are many ways to move past it and start writing. The following are some of the best strategies to help you start writing.

Write an Outline

Often it helps to write an outline and then build on that structure. Once you have a format, you can start writing from any point (which isn't necessarily at the beginning).

After writing an outline, go through the information you've gathered to determine where it best fits. You may discover you've left something out. Getting all your information organized and written down is a big step toward finishing a project. Once you have a complete outline, all you have to do is write out your thoughts in more detail. Following are examples of a standard outline format and a method for mapping out your ideas:

A. **Major Topic**
   1. **Supporting information**
   2. **Supporting information**

B. **Major Topic**
   1. **Supporting information**
      a. Detailed example
      b. Detailed example
   2. **Supporting information**
      a. Detailed example
      b. Detailed example

C. **Major Topic**
   1. **Supporting information**
   2. **Supporting information**

An example of a mindmapping diagram.

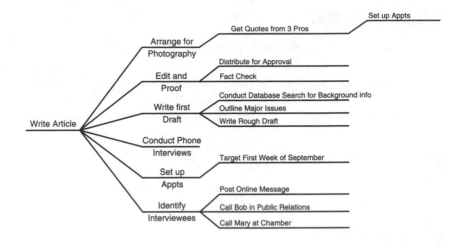

Do More Research

If you find that you're stuck, that you can't seem to find a place to start writing, perhaps you don't know enough about the subject to begin writing at all.

Tip

It pays to know the best sources when doing background research. I've found these to be particularly helpful:

➤ *Reader's Guide to Periodicals*

➤ *The U.S. Industrial Outlook*

➤ *Encyclopedia of Associations*

➤ Online search services

Your local library's business section will have all or most of these reference materials.

Instead of sitting for hours waiting for the words to materialize, consider doing more research. That may mean actually traipsing to the library, or wandering over to your boss' office and asking for some clarification on the project you're working on.

Whatever the project, take a step backward and determine what it is that you don't know. After you've figured out where you're getting confused, turn to an information source for more direction or more material.

Be careful, however, not to use research as an excuse to avoid writing. If you have enough information to write an outline, you probably are ready to begin writing. But if there are too many holes in your outline, stop and gather more data.

Force Yourself to Write Something...Anything

Sometimes writer's block is simply inertia. To get through it, you need to will yourself to start putting pen to paper, or your fingers to the keyboard. While what first appears on the page may not be Shakespeare, at least it's a start. Eventually, as you get into the flow of writing, your work will improve. Just force yourself to get some thoughts and ideas on paper. You can always edit it later!

Write Down the Facts

Instead of trying to organize all your thoughts and getting them down on paper, just focus on putting down all the relevant information you have. Use bullet points, short phrases, or incomplete sentences to get your thoughts down on paper. Write down whatever comes to mind, even if you don't know whether it really relates to the project.

Express Your Opinions

OK, if you're not sure of the facts, start with your opinions instead. How do you feel about the subject you're working on? What do others think? What are the issues on which you do and don't agree? Do you have information to support your opinion?

After you have expressed your personal thoughts, now start filling in some of the other information you know.

Start with Something Controversial

If you're having trouble identifying what's important and what's not, look for something controversial or different about your topic. What areas do people disagree on? What are your opinions on the subject?

Tip
Set up file folders labeled with project names so that you can quickly and easily collect useful information in one place. When you come across newspaper clippings, notes, or relevant tidbits that may be helpful to your assignment, just throw them in the appropriate folder. Then, when you are ready to wrap up a project, you'll find your research is almost done.

Tip
Some people start by writing something totally unrelated to the work at hand. If you can't get excited about writing about last month's sales results, write about your daughter's recent dance recital. Then once you're into the swing of writing, switch back to reporting on your sales.

Don't Try to Do Everything in One Sitting

One of the major reasons people experience writer's block is that they feel overwhelmed. Trying to start and finish a whole writing project in a short time is stressful.

Never plan to write anything longer than a couple of pages in one sitting. That way, if the words begin to flow you'll feel good about accomplishing more than you set out to do. By attempting to do too much, you put too much pressure on yourself.

The solution is to break big projects into smaller tasks of, say 10–15 minutes each. Then each day, start and finish one small piece of the whole project. Schedule time every day to work on a little piece. Suddenly it's done. The trick is not to procrastinate so that you leave the project until the last minute. Of course, this won't work if the project is due tomorrow.

A project management form.

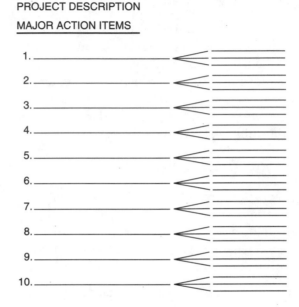

PROJECT DESCRIPTION

MAJOR ACTION ITEMS

1.
2.
3.
4.
5.
6.
7.
8.
9.
10.

Break your project down into 5-10 action items and then break each one of these actions down further into smaller to do items until you have mini-action items that take only a few minutes.

Turn to Some Idea-Generating Tools

If you have all the information you need but can't figure out how to organize it, try some creativity products to get your brain in gear.

Keep some small toys around to amuse yourself when you're feeling stressed. Many advertising agencies and creative departments decorate their offices with toys and fun pictures to help keep employees' minds stimulated.

Tip

Roger von Oech's "Creative Whack Pack" is a deck of 64 cards designed to help you get a new perspective on projects. Each card asks a question, poses a hypothetical situation for you to consider, or offers a challenge to conventional ways of dealing with situations. While it may not provide the answer to your specific challenge, it will help get your mind working again.

Michael Michalko's "ThinkPak" is a similar tool that can help individuals and groups come up with new ideas and solutions.

For example, it's hard to write a persuasive sales letter if you aren't clear on the advantages your company holds over the competition. But ThinkPak can help identify strengths you might not have thought of on your own.

Give Up

OK, if you've tried and tried and you still can't make any progress, don't waste any more time—put the project aside and do something else. Writer's block is often caused by anxiety, so try doing something relaxing and you'll be in much better shape. If you can, go for a walk, get some light exercise, or take a coffee break. If you can't, simply switch to working on a different project for a little while.

The Least You Need to Know

➤ Writer's block interferes with your productivity. Fortunately, there are many ways to become unblocked.

➤ Feeling overwhelmed and anxious often causes writer's block.

➤ There are six major types of writer's block. Identifying the cause of yours is the first step to finding a cure.

➤ Break down a project into smaller pieces. This sometimes makes the project seem less daunting and helps you get past the block.

Part 3
Standard Rules and Guidelines

Trying to write without knowing the basics of grammar, punctuation, and style is like trying to play a game without knowing the rules. You have to know how sentences are put together in order to successfully make your point just as you need to know the rules of a game in order to win.

Games are fun once you know the strategy behind them, and this chapter aims to teach you some fundamental writing strategies. In this section, you'll learn how to correctly structure sentences and use punctuation symbols. You'll also hear about writing style and tone, which you can use to communicate more effectively with your reader.

Grammar

"Ugh!" you're saying to yourself as you look at this chapter. "How boring can you get?" OK, I'll agree with you. Grammar isn't the most sexy topic, but it is actually one of the most important.

Grammar goof-ups are so obvious that readers will focus more on any mistakes you've made and less on the content of your message. So unless you want to draw attention where it's not wanted, you'll be wise to skim through this chapter.

Grammar Basics

Let's start with the basic elements of a sentence. You always have a noun, the person, place, or thing you're writing about, and a verb, the word suggesting what kind of action is taking place.

Definition

Sentence Fragment An incomplete sentence that is missing either a noun or a verb, or just doesn't communicate a whole thought. For example, "she waits for" has both a noun and a verb, but it still isn't complete.

In addition to nouns and verbs, your sentences should also have adjectives and adverbs. Adjectives give more detail about the noun in your sentence and adverbs give more detail about the verb.

Quote

Avoid using always, never, all, none, and other extremes. They usually are not accurate because there are exceptions to every case.

Dr. Ernie Stech, Chief Mountain Consulting, Inc. in Littleton, Colorado.

For example, "Mary paced the hallway nervously waiting for the board of director's decision." In that sentence, "Mary" is a noun; she is the subject of the sentence. "Hallway," "board of directors," and "decision" are other nouns that are secondary. "Paced" and "waiting" are verbs indicating some kind of action, and "nervously" is an adverb describing how Mary paced.

Don't get too caught up in analyzing sentence structure. Just be aware that every sentence must have a subject and verb. Adverbs and adjectives are also frequently used, but aren't required for a sentence to be correct.

Pronouns

Pronouns are references to people—I, you, she, he, we, and they. Sometimes a pronoun is either accompanied by or replaced by an antecedent, which is a word that the pronoun refers to. For instance, in the sentence "John saw Sue in the cafeteria and went over to talk with her," "her" is an antecedent referring back to Sue.

There are clear linkages between the two, and as soon as you know the rules, you'll be less likely to misuse pronouns and antecedents:

Pronoun	Antecedent
I	Me, myself, mine
You	You, yours
He	Him, his
She	Her, hers
We	Us, our
You (plural)	You, theirs

Tip

There, their, and they're are three different ways of spelling a word that sounds exactly alike, and are often used incorrectly. "There" refers to a place. "Their" refers to a group's possession of something (it belongs to them). "They're" means "they are."

These pronouns and antecedents go together and can't be used interchangeably. If you use the word "she" in your sentence, you know any reference back to that person must be either "her" or "hers." Any other antecedent would be wrong.

Quote

If you're not sure whether to use "me" or "I," take the other person out of the sentence and say it out loud to hear if it sounds right. For example, take "Jim and" out of this sentence: "This gift is from (Jim and) I." "This gift is from I" doesn't sound right, so you know the correct word is "me."

Sandra Beckwith, author of *Why Can't a Man Be More Like a Woman?*

Agreement

When the subject in your sentence is in sync with the verb, you have agreement. To determine if you have agreement, you need to look at whether your subject is singular or plural and whether your verb is singular or plural.

For example, "The food service workers looks through the proposed contract," would be incorrect. Your subject, the food service workers, is plural. So your verb must also be plural. "Look" or "looked," depending on whether you are writing in present or past tense, would be correct.

When writing, think about the subject in your sentence. Then form the verb that goes with that noun and use it. Sometimes when the subject and verb are at opposite ends of a sentence, it gets confusing as to exactly what the subject is. And that's usually when the incorrect verb is used. Always refer back to the subject for a double-check.

Tip
Keep your sentences to fewer than 17 words to reduce the chance of a run-on sentence.

Problems with parallel sentences also come into play when you have a list of items. For example, a list of your CEO's most notable achievements.

During her tenure at XYZ Company, Carol has:

➤ <u>Computerized</u> the entire company

➤ <u>Established</u> a training department

➤ <u>Increased</u> sales by 250%

Notice how all three items at the start of each line are verbs in the past tense. The key is to be consistent in how you begin each line. If you start the first sentence with a verb, you need to be consistent in starting the rest of your items with verbs. And be sure they are all in the same tense. The following would not be parallel, however:

Our goals for the coming year are to:

➤ Improve productivity

➤ Increasing the size of the board of directors

➤ Have introduced two new products

The items in this list are not parallel, so it sounds funny, doesn't it? You need to use either verbs in the future tense (such as improve), verbs ending in "ing" (such as increasing), or verbs in the past tense (such as have introduced).

You don't have to start each element on the list with a verb; nouns and adjectives are fine, too. The trick is simply sticking with one format, whichever you choose.

Verb Tenses

When writing for business, frequently you're speaking in the present tense. That means everything that is happening is happening now or in the very near future. When you're unsure of which tense to use, revert to the present tense.

When writing proposals recommending that certain actions be taken, typically you are writing in the future tense. You want your prospect to take some action in the future that will benefit both companies.

Reports, on the other hand, are generally always written in the past tense. You are analyzing events that have already occurred, so even if the purpose is to suggest a future course of action, the tense of the report is still the past.

Letters are frequently written in the present or past tense, which depends on the reason for your correspondence. If you are writing to comment on something someone has done—good or bad—you would write in the past tense. If you are writing to ask that something be done, you would switch to the future tense towards the end of your letter, when you ask for a response. Sales letters are typically written in the present tense because much of what you are telling the reader is about your current capabilities and reasons they should buy (and buy now, not later).

Memos can be written in the past, present, or future tense. Press releases announcing an upcoming event are written in the future tense, unless the event or announcement has already occurred, in which case the past tense would be appropriate. Articles are often written in the past tense, especially if you are writing about a client who has used your company's services.

> **Quote**
> Be sure you know the difference between "its" and "it's." "It's" always means "it is."
>
> **Deborah Layton**, Senior Associate Director of Planned Giving at the University of Pennsylvania.

> **Tip**
> A document sounds "choppy" when you use too many short sentences in quick succession. Vary the length of your sentences to make your document flow better and sound more professional.

Numbers

Numbers are also frequently written out incorrectly. No one is quite sure whether you're supposed to use numerals or letters when talking about numbers. But there are actually rules for when to use the actual numbers and when to use words.

When using any number between one and ten, you should write it out just as you see it here. If you write about the seven new products your company is introducing or the four new employees who have been hired, you need to write out the numbers. If you wrote "7 new products" or "4 new hires," you would be wrong. Anything ten or under is written out.

By the same token, all numbers greater than ten are written as numbers. So although ten is always expressed as "ten," 11, 12, 13 and so on are written numerically.

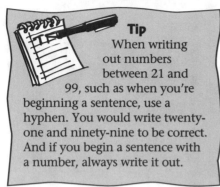

Tip

When writing out numbers between 21 and 99, such as when you're beginning a sentence, use a hyphen. You would write twenty-one and ninety-nine to be correct. And if you begin a sentence with a number, always write it out.

Unfortunately, there are exceptions. It couldn't be that simple, could it?! Whenever you begin a sentence with a number, no matter what it is, you have to write it out. The sentence "15 sandwiches were stolen from the refrigerator" is wrong;" "Fifteen sandwiches were stolen from the refrigerator" is how it should be written. If you have another number(s) appearing after the first number, follow the normal rules depending on whether the number is more or less than ten. Some other rules to be aware of are:

➤ Dollar amounts should always be written as numbers ($100, $5, $3.50).

➤ Percentages are also expressed as numbers (21%, 8%, 250%).

➤ Measurements should be written numerically (3×5 card, 12 foot long wall, 60 yards).

➤ When referring to a number, use the number itself ("write a 1, 2, or 3 on the survey...").

Quote

The words "over" and "more than" are often used interchangeably when they have different meanings. "Over" means on top of, while "more than" means greater than. So writing "the company's earnings were over $2 billion in 1996" is wrong. It should read "the company's earnings were more than $2 billion."

Michael Bloch, Publisher of *Business Strategies Newspaper*.

The Least You Need to Know

➤ Letters, memos, proposals, reports, and press materials are typically written in a specific verb tense.

➤ Pronouns all have a corresponding antecedent that should always be used with it.

➤ If your subject noun is singular, be sure the tense of your verb is singular as well. For a plural noun, you need a plural verb. Hint: A singular verb usually ends in "s."

➤ Numbers from one to ten should be written out in word format while numbers greater than ten should be written as numerals.

Chapter 11

Punctuation

In This Chapter

➤ Commas are the pauses in your sentences

➤ Preventing run-on sentences

➤ Possessive pitfalls

➤ Using parentheses

Although you may not have paid all that much attention to rules of punctuation in grade school, punctuation can make the difference between good writing and poor writing. Just think about the impression you're given when you read something that is full of punctuation errors; you wonder about the professionalism of the person who wrote it, don't you? Well, don't let this happen to you.

Becoming more familiar with some of the basic punctuation rules can significantly improve your writing. Just learning when to and when not to use commas, for example, can impact how well you write. Other punctuation marks, like exclamation points, periods, colons and semicolons ensure that your sentences don't all run together nonsensically. Imagine what a mess you would have without symbols that signify when a sentence has ended, or when a new point is being made. The trick is learning when to use them.

How Punctuation Makes a Difference

Punctuation marks add meaning and expression to our writing. They help us understand when an important point is being made or when a question is being asked, in addition to keeping order within our sentences.

Mistakes cause us to read sentences incorrectly or to misunderstand what the author is trying to say. To avoid these problems, brush up on some of the general rules of punctuation.

Commas

A comma has several roles. One is to join independent groups of words together so that they make sense. Another is to clarify a point. And a third is to separate essential from nonessential information in a sentence.

When you read a sentence and come across a comma, what is your natural instinct? You want to pause. Well, that's one way that commas should be used in your sentences. Read through what you've written and look for places where you want the reader to pause slightly. Put a comma there.

There are also specific words that require a comma before or after them, depending on how they're being used. These include:

➤ **and**   Tom, Sally, and John attended the meeting.

➤ **but**   The proposal was well written and thought out, but the company just doesn't have the budget for it.

➤ **or**   We could buy either a copier, printer, or a combination of the two.

➤ **nor**   Neither Ann, Jennifer, nor Josh could support the proposed layoffs.

➤ **for**   Susan B. Anthony was a feminist, for she believed in the rights of women.

➤ **yet**   He had excellent references, yet he lacked sales experience.

Commas are also used to separate lists of items. For example, "You could select the prime rib, lobster, or chicken for lunch today." To figure out how many commas you should have, just subtract one from however many items on your list. If you have three items to list, you need two commas. Likewise, if you have five things to mention, you'll need four commas in your sentence.

Another place where you'll need a comma is whenever you have an introductory clause of five words or more, (like this one) you should use a comma right after it. If your introductory clause has fewer than five words, you don't need to add one.

Apostrophes

Those little upside down commas hanging in the air above certain letters are apostrophes, which some people have a hard time figuring out when to use. It's actually quite easy. There are only two times you need to remember to use an apostrophe: when you're forming a contraction and when you're indicating possession of something.

Definition
Contraction
When two words are joined together to form one, with some letters eliminated in the process. Wherever the letters are removed, the apostrophe is put in its place.

Indicate Missing Letters or Numbers

Use an apostrophe when contracting two words. For example, the word "don't" is a contraction of the words "do" and "not." The two words are smooshed together and the second "o" is taken out and replaced by an apostrophe. "Can't" is another contraction, as is "they're," short for "they are."

Only certain words can be made into contractions. Generally, two words where the second word is "not" or "are" are good candidates for contracting.

Apostrophes also indicate when numbers have been eliminated, such as in '96 instead of 1996.

Indicate Possession

The only other time an apostrophe is used is when you want to express possession of something. For instance, if John owns a car, you would write that the car is John's. An apostrophe followed by an "s" communicates that the car belongs to John. Since John is a singular noun, you simply add an apostrophe and an "s."

Be careful, however, when you're dealing with several items or people. A family, for example, would be plural because it consists of several people. With a plural noun, the rule is that you add an "s" after the item and then an apostrophe; the reverse of how you write a singular possessive noun. So if a family's last name was Turner, you would write the Turners' car.

In situations where the noun already ends in "s", you just tack on the apostrophe. The word "class" would be one instance where you would simply add an apostrophe to the word: "The eleventh grade class' social service project was...." You don't need to add an extra "s" anywhere, just the apostrophe.

Exclamation Points

Like periods and question marks, exclamation points end sentences. Periods indicate that you've finished making a point, question marks end a question that you've posed, and exclamation points are really just periods with enthusiasm.

If you want to emphasize a point or suggest that you're really excited about something you've just written, end your sentence with an exclamation point.

Tip

When making a point by asking a question, use both a question mark followed by an exclamation point. For example, "Why did she even consider moving the company to Guam when our customer base is in New York City?!" asks a question that you don't really expect to get an answer to. You're really commenting more than asking.

Since business writing is typically more formal than personal letter writing, you'll want to avoid overusing exclamation points. They were cute in high school when you punctuated sentences with several at a time, but now you don't want to appear too eager (or juvenile).

Tip
Underline, capitalize, or italicize the names of books, magazines, newspapers, and other published works.

As a general guideline, one or two exclamation points per page is plenty. If you have more, you weaken the impact of all of them. They should be used sparingly, when you want to highlight something good that's happened or something you're concerned about. But don't use them regularly.

Quotation Marks

When you quote someone or something, like a book or report, you're repeating exactly what someone else said. And since you don't want to take credit for something someone else said, you use quotation marks around her statements to indicate they're not your words.

Quotation marks are two little upside down commas dangling before and after a series of words: " and ". You type a set of quotation marks when you begin repeating something someone else said and then you type another set when you end the statement.

So if you wanted to alert people in your office, for instance, that they should cut back on their use of exclamation points, you could write: Marcia Layton points out that "one or two exclamation points per page is plenty." If you didn't want to write exactly what I said, but wanted to summarize it, you wouldn't need to use quotation marks. They're used only when you're repeating exactly what someone said or wrote.

Tip
Use quotation marks around the titles of magazine or newspaper articles or reports, followed by the underlined name of the magazine or newspaper itself.

Tip
Punctuation marks, such as commas and periods, should go before the ending quotation mark, not after. This is one area where mistakes are often made. "Ice cream is a major food group," is correct. "Ice cream is a major food group". is not.

When you report something someone else said within a quote, you use single quotation marks (which look strikingly like apostrophes). For example, "The VP of marketing told our department that we were 'extremely talented employees.'" Notice at the end of the sentence you have both sets of single and double quotation marks. That's because quotation marks always come in pairs. There is always one at the beginning and one at the end. You should never leave one hanging.

Tip
When listing someone's college or graduate degrees after their names, capitalize them. But don't capitalize them when writing about the degree itself. For example, "Doug Snyder, MBA" would be correct, but "master of business administration" doesn't need capitalization.

Hyphens and Parentheses

Whenever you want to add some supplementary information that isn't quite as important, you can use either parentheses, commas, or a hyphen. Parentheses are those sideway semi-circles that also come in pairs and look like this ( ).

Whenever you need to clarify a point, or mention some extra information that isn't crucial to what you're trying to say, put the information within parentheses.

For example, "Bob was looking at three different cars (a BMW, Lexus, and Mercedes) to replace his aging Porsche." We don't really need to know which three cars he's considering, but it is interesting extra information to have. The sentence still makes sense without the three cars mentioned, so we put them within parentheses.

That's really the key—does the sentence make sense without the extra information? If the answer is yes, you should either put parentheses, commas, or hyphens around the information. If the answer is no, the sentence does not make sense without the information, then you shouldn't use any punctuation marks to set it apart.

Parentheses are frequently used to provide supplemental information while commas and hyphens are used as a way to offset the additional detail. When using hyphens in this manner, it is correct to use two together, like this: —. Another option is to use a single em dash.

Parentheses and commas are actually more common ways to offset supplementary information, but hyphens are becoming more frequently used because they tend not to visually break up the flow of the sentence as much.

Tip

There is a difference between a hyphen, which looks like this (-) and an em dash, which is a little longer (—). Hyphens are used to join two words, such as twenty-one and user-friendly, while em dashes are used to join phrases, often replacing parentheses, as in: The company was bankrupt—creditors had been calling for weeks—though the offical papers hadn't been filed yet.

Colons and Semicolons

Colons and semicolons are used to provide follow-up or additional information after a sentence, without causing a run-on sentence. Sometimes it's hard to tell when a colon is correct and when a semicolon is correct, so I'll try to clear that up for you here.

Colons

Colons look like two periods right on top of one another (:) and are used to indicate that you're going to give more information after it. That extra information is either a list or some kind of explanation.

For example, "Sarah had to purchase several items for her new business with her severance money: a desk, phone, fax machine, and copier." The list of items she needs to buy comes immediately after the statement to that effect, providing additional information.

Semicolons

Semicolons break up run-on sentences. They're used to separate two independent thoughts—when no conjunction is used—but still suggest that they're related.

A period clearly separates two different statements and suggests that they have almost nothing to do with each other. A semicolon, on the other hand, is used when you want to follow up a first statement with some kind of example or clarifier. For example: "Sentences full of errors look sloppy; editors often circle and underline the mistakes in red ink."

Semicolons are very similar to colons, but are used in situations where you're providing additional information that isn't in the form of a list or explanation. In those situations you would use a colon; in all others you use a semicolon.

The Least You Need to Know

➤ Without punctuation marks, writing would be just a jumbled mixture of words. Punctuation adds meaning.

➤ Periods, question marks, and exclamation points are all used to end sentences, with exclamation points used only sparingly, if at all.

➤ Commas are used to join groups of words together to form a sentence. Look for places where you would pause if you were speaking; that's where a comma should go.

➤ Quotation marks are used to indicate that you are repeating verbatim what someone else has said or written.

➤ Semicolons and colons allow you to add a follow-up statement onto the end of a sentence, without causing a run-on.

General Style Issues

Up to this point we've been talking about content—the information you're writing about. And a little later in this book you'll learn some formatting tips to improve the appearance of your documents. Right now, however, it's important that you understand that the way you express yourself impacts how your message is received.

No matter what the words on the page say, if the format or tone of your memo or letter suggests a different message, your readers will most likely believe what they want to believe. If there's any confusion about what you're really trying to say, people will read into your document things you probably never meant.

How Style Impacts the Reader

If you send out a letter to your staff explaining that no one can take a vacation during the months of July or August, you're telling them something they don't want to hear. Most people take time off during the two warmest months of the summer and being told that they can't is not good news.

Their first reaction may be, "She can't be serious." Or, "I'm sure this doesn't apply to everyone, probably just some people (but certainly not me)." So they'll try to gauge how serious you are by looking at other aspects of your letter. They'll scrutinize the tone of your words—are you laying down the law, or testing the waters?

What your letter looks like will also suggest whether your reader should believe you or not—is it brief or do you go overboard in explaining why this has to be done and apologizing for any inconvenience? The more words there are, the worse you must feel, and the better their chances of changing your mind.

Formatting also plays a role. Is your document a casual informational memo or a formal letter from the higher-ups?

All of these subtle clues help your reader fully understand your message.

You've undoubtedly heard the saying, "Do as I say, not as I do," which implies that sometimes our words don't match our actions. This is exactly the point I want to make.

Be careful of how your words appear on the printed page, or people will ignore what you've said and focus more on how you've said it. In some cases, people will discount the content of your message and choose to believe what they think your tone and style suggests. So be as consistent as possible in what you say and how you get your point across.

> **Quote**
> It's refreshing to use a short sentence(s) for an opening—"it builds speed," my writing teacher would say.
>
> Sentence fragments can do the same thing, and are more common in speech. They make the flow more conversational, which seems to be the trend in writing these days.
>
> **Jennifer Harrison**, freelance writer and editor, Indianapolis, Indiana.

Does Your Writing Sound Like You Wrote It?

We all have our own style of speaking and communicating that makes us unique. The pace at which we speak, the way we enunciate certain words and use others so frequently that they become a sort of trademark, are all part of our personalities and personal styles of communicating.

Think about the comedians who mimic famous people, exaggerating their movements, accent, and way of speaking in a humorous way. Of course, we know exactly who they're pretending to be because of those recognizable clues. Those famous people are memorable because of their quirks and unique mannerisms.

And so it is with writing. The more you write, the more you develop your own personal style that becomes recognizable to others.

Newspaper columnists who write regularly for the daily papers each have their own style and mood that endear us to them. Some we read religiously and others we could just as well do without. They're all writing about important matters, but how they address different issues affects whether we want to read them or not.

Think about how you respond to people verbally when you have good and bad news to tell them. And how do you react when you're in a good mood? How are you different when you're in a bad mood? Everyone can tell when you're in a bad mood; think about what gives it away.

> **Quote**
> In every fat book there is a thin book trying to get out.
>
> **Unknown**

> **Tip**
> Taking a firm stand on an issue helps your audience understand your commitment to it. Eliminate any wishy-washy words such as "sort of" or "fairly."

If you're worried about writing the way you speak because you're concerned about how well you express yourself verbally, keep in mind that in writing, you can always edit. When you're speaking, you don't have the option to go back and correct your pronunciation or take out the harsh tone of voice you use. Fortunately, with the written word, you can write down your ideas and then go back several times, improving your message each time.

Setting aside a sensitive document is also a good idea, especially when you're emotional. When we get angry, everyone has a tendency to write (and speak) with a lot of hostility. Or when we're sad, for example, we may get a little too mushy for the business world.

Whenever you write something in an emotional state, don't send it off immediately. Put it away at least overnight and look at it again the next morning. You may decide to tone down some of the words you used, or take some out altogether. Be sure that what you send out isn't something you'll be embarrased by next week, or next month.

Before you begin to write a document that has a particular tone or mood to it, pretend you are speaking to the people this is going out to. How would you go about telling them this information? Visualize yourself in front of them, talking with them. Now write down exactly how you would tell them. The closer you are to writing what you would verbally say, the more your own personality and style become part of your writing.

What Is the Mood of Your Message?

How you convey the mood of your message is done primarily through the words you choose. Length and thoroughness are other factors.

The more you write, the more open to discussion you appear to be. Your audience may imagine that you want to get all the issues in the open so you can get feedback. This is generally the case with documents like internal employee newsletters or company annual reports. You want to provide information, but you also want to stimulate discussion and thinking.

On the other hand, when you are providing information about a decision that has already been made, you want to be more brief. Explain the situation, comment on what's being done about it, and leave it at that. The less you say, the less feedback you'll get. So just by writing in as few words as possible, you're communicating that the information is not negotiable. Your position is clear and you're merely reporting on what has already been decided.

Quote
Whether you're writing a memo or report, think Hemingway, not Faulkner. Use short sentences that make your point quickly and clearly.

Sandra Beckwith, Owner, Beckwith Communications.

As you start to write, decide first whether you want to generate feedback or just inform your audience.

Typically in a sales situation, you want as much feedback as possible. Whether you're submitting a proposal or an initial sales letter to build interest in your company's products, you want to hear back from the recipient of your letter or proposal. So you'll provide a thorough picture of your product, what it can do for your customers, and why people should buy it. You'll also let your reader know that you welcome comments.

By giving people all the basic information they need to evaluate your product or company, but not too much in the way of specifics, you're inviting follow-up contact. You want to answer those questions and take those calls. You welcome it.

When delivering good news, such as patting someone on the back for a job well done or reporting record sales this month, you want to get the word out to everyone. Distributing the good news far and wide serves two purposes: it helps reinforce your company's image as a good business, and it really makes the people who are responsible for the good news feel important and special. Recognition is worth more than money to most employees, so take every opportunity to share good news.

Generally a letter or memo, depending on whether you're communicating internally or externally, is the appropriate document type to use. Specifics are also important when reporting good news. You want everyone to understand exactly what the good news is, why it's good news, who was responsible. and how it happened. Don't just say "Thanks to our accounting team, the company saved $2 million this month on office supplies." Instead, say "Thanks to the 12 members of our accounting team, who smartly negotiated better credit terms with our office supply company, we saved $2 million this month."

By the same token, when you're reporting bad news you want to maintain control of the information flow. You want to distribute information to whomever it needs to go to but without causing a frenzy. For instance, if you've just learned that your CEO has resigned and you need to tell the board of directors, you want to issue some sort of memo right away. The point is to alert them to the situation and give them all the basic information you have so that they can start to make some decisions. Or if your company is closing down a plant, you want to tell all the employees first. Then you'll want to tell the shareholders and the media.

In the information you're providing, you want to be clear and brief, giving them all the details they need without going overboard and revealing all the internal discussions around the issue. They just need to know what's happening and why. So that's all you should be telling them until you have more information available.

Keep in mind that even when delivering bad news, you can soften the blow by starting off with the positives of the situation. OK, you may need to stretch your imagination to find the good news, but it's there. By stating some good news first, or emphasizing the positives of the particular situation, you avoid getting your reader immediately on the defensive.

For example, if you've noticed that everyone on your staff has been leaving at 4:30 pm instead of 5:00 pm, when the day is officially done, you may want to remind them of normal working hours. But don't start by accusing people of leaving early; that will just get their guard up. Rather, begin by complimenting everyone on some of the projects they've recently finished, or on their productivity level. But then remind them in a nice way that they're needed in the office util 5:00 pm to make some real headway on a new project, or to be available to take phone calls from customers, for example.

The key is to back into bad news by highlighting something positive. Ending on a positive note is also smart, so that your reader feels good about what you've asked him or her to do, rather than being in a bad mood.

The Least You Need to Know

➤ Visualize yourself talking to your audience and write exactly what you would tell them in person.

➤ The closer you are to writing how you speak, the more of your own personality you communicate in your writing.

➤ Your attitude comes through in how you format your document, how much detail you provide, and the tone of your words.

➤ If you tend to write more than you need to—giving more detail than necessary—you may appear to be defensive about your message. Editing is the solution.

Part 4
Presentation Basics

Everything you write should follow the standard spelling, grammatical, and punctuation rules—that's a given. But what your documents look like visually also makes a big impact on the reader.

This section will teach you how to make your pages easy to read and follow, as well as help you emphasize important points and downplay others. Formatting and design tricks improve the effectiveness of anything you write, so become familiar with these techniques. You'll improve the quality of your writing even more.

Chapter 13

Improved Readability

In This Chapter

➤ Using headers to lead the reader

➤ Choosing the right typestyle

➤ The ultimate management tool—bullet points

➤ Tips to control length

If you've ever heard the term "white space" when referring to a printed piece, you're probably familiar with the importance of what a document looks like beyond the words on the page. White space is the area on a page not filled with words and graphics—essentially, wherever it's blank. The more white space you leave on a page, the easier it is for your eyes to distinguish all the words and letters.

Think about how you instinctively react to two different pages: one that looks like it has about 200 words on it and another that seems to have every nook and cranny of space filled with letters. Which one do you think you're more likely to want to read? Exactly. The one that looks like it will be less painful to get through, the one with only 200 words.

Because we're all pressed for time, we tend to put aside tasks that will take longer than a few minutes. But we'll react immediately to activities that can be finished quickly. We don't want to get bogged down with reading something that's going to take half an hour or more. Be mindful of your audience's lack of time and try to create documents that look easy to get through. What does "easy" look like? Easy is something that doesn't take a lot of brain power to understand. You should be able to grasp the meaning within a matter of minutes.

Don't Scare Your Readers Off

What prevents people from diving right in and reading something important that lands on their desk? Often what the document looks like has a lot to do with it. Your challenge as a writer is to make your documents as short as possible, using a legible font, highlighting the most important points in some way.

Definition

Font   A term for what the letters on your computer or typewriter look like. There are thousands of different fonts, or typestyles, that affect how large or small the letters are, whether they are simple or fancy, and the image they project.

Discouraging Readers

To avoid scaring away your audience when they look at your memo or report, follow these guidelines:

➤ Don't use a small font (10 points or less).

➤ Don't use a lot of long paragraphs; use headers to break up text.

➤ Don't use more than 2 or 3 fonts in a document.

➤ Don't make your writing appear crowded with single spacing; one and a half spacing is easier to read.

➤ Don't crowd all the text into margins of less than an inch.

When someone first picks up your document, they're evaluating how urgent it is. What's it about? How soon do they have to read it? And, how long will it take to get through it? Even if you have the most urgent document on the face of the earth, chances are good that if it looks like it's going to take more than 10 minutes to read, it will be put aside. Yes, this is probably very frustrating for you. But if you try and avoid the four don'ts listed previously, you'll be in good shape.

Headers

One step you can take to make reading your documents easier and more pleasing is to use headers. Headers are phrases or titles that introduce the topic of the upcoming paragraph. Often they appear in bold, or underlined, to set them apart from the other paragraphs.

For example, if you're writing about the advantages of telecommuting (working from home and communicating with the office by phone), some of the headers might be: Improved productivity, Reduced sicktime, Lower operating costs, Higher employee morale, and so on. Each of these headers would be featured on its own line just before the paragraph(s) dedicated to each of those topics. In addition to serving as a mini-introduction to the topic, it also visually leads the reader through the document; the headers in bold emphasize the major points even without having to read the paragraphs themselves.

Which Typestyle Is Best

Studies have shown that serif fonts are easier for the eyes to read. Apparently we're more used to seeing serif type fonts, so our brains can interpret them faster when we're reading. Below, the font on the left is a serif font, and the font on the right is a sans serif font.

A	A
Garamond	Helvetica

There is no standard font that everyone uses, though there are some that are more popular than others. It appears that these are the ones that come with most computer programs, so we get used to using them on a regular basis.

Despite the lack of standard in what the font looks like, a ten or twelve point size is a standard. Larger sized fonts are used for headers or for emphasizing important points within a document, but not as the typical text font. And smaller than 10 point gets tough to read. You'll definitely get complaints from folks who are farsighted if you insist on tiny type.

Interestingly, most major corporations have corporate colors and a corporate typeface. Sound silly? It's not. Your organization's image and reputation are built on a lot of different impressions people have of the company. These impressions are affected by what the logo looks like, the colors that are used in the

Tip
Some of the most popular fonts are Palatino, Bodoni, and Times.

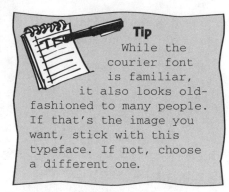

Tip

While the courier font is familiar, it also looks old-fashioned to many people. If that's the image you want, stick with this typeface. If not, choose a different one.

Tip

Less is more. When in doubt, keep it short.

product packaging and ads, and the typestyle that appears in the literature.

Check with your boss to see if there is a particular font that she or he prefers that you use. Or pull out a memo that someone has recently sent you and try and identify which font they used.

Even if your organization doesn't have a standard font it uses in its marketing, there are probably fonts that they prefer to see.

Before computers, most typewriters came with one or two different typestyles. Courier was one of the popular ones, which is still used by some people who want to present a homespun image; as if they really did type this individual sheet on a typewriter. In general, I wouldn't recommend Courier for that reason—it looks like you used a type-writer instead of a computer.

Controlling Length

If you're only allowed to turn in a certain number of pages, there are several tricks you can use to change the length of your document.

Font Size and Style

Interestingly, the type of font you choose can drastically affect how long your page is. Even if they look identical on your computer screen, two different fonts will print very differently on your printer.

Generally, serif fonts will take up more space on the page. *Serifs* are those curly endings on the edge of letters. Sans serif fonts are the ones without the curly endings; they are very plain and kind of futuristic looking. Typically, they take up less space.

Font style has little to do with the actual size that you choose to make your letters. Font size 10 or 12 are the most frequently used for everyday writing, with 12 being preferred because it's easier on the eyes.

Reducing and Enlarging the Page

Just about every computer word-processing program has a feature that allows you to shrink the page a little, or enlarge it up to 200% of the current size.

You can make a one and a half page document squeeze into a single page, if necessary. But don't go overboard. Of course, you can squeeze four pages onto one if you had to, but no one would be able to read it because the type would be so teeny tiny. Be reasonable about how much you're trying to fudge.

The steps involved in reducing the size of your page are simple. Step one: Find the reduction and enlargement feature, which is usually part of the "page setup" function. Reduce it from 100% to 95% by typing **95** and see what happens. The object is to have everything fit on the page, with the type as large as possible.

Sometimes you'll need to go back and reset it at a smaller number, such as 90%, to get everything to fit. Or you may find that you can enlarge the page a little closer to 100% and still make it work. Try 96%, 97%, and so on until all the words are on the page and it's legible.

If you're typing on a manual typewriter, you're out of luck, unless you want to literally cut and paste the paper together. It's a bit trickier with a typewriter, but it can still be done as long as you also have a photocopier nearby.

What you need to do is type your document, reduce it on the copier by 90% or so, and then try pasting it onto a regular 8 1/2 × 11 inch piece of paper. Does it all fit? If not, you'll need to adjust your reduction percentages and try again. Keep those scissors and tape handy because you may be awhile.

Justifying

Sometimes how your page is justified can affect the length of your document. Left justified paragraphs, where the words are lined up straight on the left and have a jagged edge on the right, can appear longer than fully justified paragraphs, where the words are lined up straight on both sides. It probably won't have a huge effect, but if you just need to shave off a line or two, give it a try.

Highlight your document and then press the appropriate button to test what left justified and justified looks like. Whichever one results in the shorter length is the one you should go with.

Margins

The white space that you leave around the edges of your document is the margin, and you can set a different width for any of the four edges if you're using a computer. Most people choose the same width for the left and right sides and vary the top and bottom margins. We'll get into some specifics about margins in a minute. I just wanted to point out that margins are one place where you can make adjustments that affect the length of what you're writing.

Now that you know the secrets of making your document appear shorter, you can also reverse the instructions if you want to turn in something that seems a little longer than what you currently have.

How Wide Are Those Margins?

The white border around a page of text is called the margin, which is typically set at one inch all around. Any less of a margin and your page will look very cramped with words.

Adjusting the size of your margins is one of the best ways to alter the length of your document, should you need to. Increasing the size of your margin from one inch to an inch and a half, for instance, pushes your text to the middle of the page. By making the document thinner, you're also making it longer. The opposite is also true.

Indenting half and inch to offset an important point, financial information, or bullet points is a standard practice. But this doesn't affect the margin for the document.

If you're creating a newsletter or a document that will have more than one column of text, you may need to change your margins so that the page looks attractive. Typically, with several columns, you'll want your margins to be smaller.

Some examples of one-, two-, and three-column formatting.

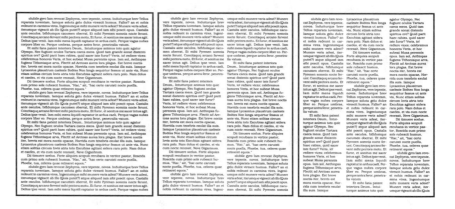

While one column is the standard format for most documents, anything similar to a publication, such as a regular bulletin, company magazine, or newsletter, is usually shown with several columns. It's actually easier to read information that is broken into multiple columns, rather than in a single one in the middle of the page.

Management Loves Bullet Points

Whether you use perfectly round little dots before your phrases or some other symbol, those dots are called bullet points. You've probably heard people talk about a "bulleted" presentation or outline, which is a reference to how the material will be layed out. For example, look at the bulleted list in "The Least You Need to Know" section at the end of this chapter.

Emphasize Key Points

Bullet points are the preferred way to highlight important pieces of information, making them stand out on the page. Your eye is attracted to the dark little dot, which causes you to read what comes after it.

A Summary Tool

Bullets also force the writer to summarize a complete sentence or point into a short phrase. This is why you'll frequently see overhead presentations made with a series of bullet points and phrases.

If you've ever had the assignment of turning a 20-page proposal into a five-cell overhead presentation, you understand why bullet points are a lifesaver. There is no way you can smoosh 20 pages into five without losing a lot of meaning. But by converting whole sentences into short descriptive phrases, you can make your point just as well. For example, the following sentence can be turned into a bullet point easily, cutting out several unnecessary words:

"The CEO of ABC Company has determined that employee benefits should be offered to unmarried partners of its employees, should they so choose to take advantage of it."

➤ Unmarried partners now entitled to full employee benefits

Or:

➤ Full benefits for unmarried partners

How short your bullet points can be depends a lot on how much other background information you're giving.

For instance, if you're providing a report on the company's benefit offerings for this year, you could have a series of bullet points highlighting the changes that have been made. But you'd need to have an introductory paragraph first to explain the topic of your report before jumping into the bullet points. Without that introduction, the bullets sometimes mean nothing to the reader; they can be too general.

Dots or Symbols

Bullet points don't have to be just round dots—you can use any small symbol to start off your line. Hyphens are popular, as are check marks and arrows. If you have a collection of different fonts, you can try squiggly marks and triangles, too. Following are examples of different bullet symbols you can use:

The one rule you need to follow, however, is to pick one type of symbol to be used as a bullet point and stick with it throughout the document. Don't use bullets in one place, arrows in another, and check marks somewhere else. Your reader may think that there's a difference of importance or priority between the different items when you may have been trying to show some creativity. Be consistent and avoid confusion.

How to Condense Content

When you find that you have scads of information and you don't want to discourage your reader from reviewing it all, you'll want to use all of the strategies we've just gone through to make it appear shorter. These include:

➤ Using headers to break up lots of text

➤ Shortening full sentences into bullet points

➤ Reducing your margins a little to get more on a page

➤ Using the page reduction feature to shrink the whole page a little

➤ Changing the font you're using to a smaller style, such as Garamand or Times

➤ Testing the page justify command to see if fully justified makes a difference

In addition to all of these tricks, there's editing. Yes, it's more work, but you should always double-check to see if you've used more words than you really needed to. If that's the case, you can condense your content by removing unnecessary words.

The Least You Need to Know

➤ White space makes your document more pleasing to the eye—don't try to cram too much in.

➤ Changing the type and size of your font will make your document appear longer or shorter.

➤ Bullet points are used to highlight important issues or facts.

➤ To fit your text into a certain number of pages, use the "reduce/enlarge" feature in your word-processing program.

➤ Headlines help introduce new topics to your reader.

➤ If layout tricks won't work, revert to good old-fashioned editing to shorten your document.

Chapter 14

When to Use Graphics

In This Chapter

➤ How to make your writing more interesting

➤ Knowing which type of chart and graph to use

➤ Other tools to help you communicate more clearly

Sometimes getting your point across can be a challenge. For whatever reason, words alone are sometimes just not enough. And, you just can't put the words together in such a way that people will understand what the heck you're talking about. This often happens when you're trying to explain a complex concept, or report on several issues or topics. Some people are immediately turned off when any kind of numbers are mentioned, which means you have to find new ways to get your audience to keep reading.

Definition
Graphics
Symbols and visual elements that help break up a document. Graphs, charts, illustrations, photographs, and typographical symbols such as bullet points are all graphics.

Visual tools, such as charts, graphs, illustrations, photographs, and small pieces of artwork, help people visually move through a letter or report. Instead of being bored by pages and pages of text, readers are much more likely to stick with a document that has interesting "pictures." These pictures are generally referred to as graphics.

Graphics have a way of highlighting the most important points, helping to emphasize what's really critical. They can also help to lump similar subjects together for clarity.

Charting Your Way to Success

One type of graphic that is frequently used to quickly communicate business information is the chart, which is a diagram used to display information in terms of lines and points on a piece of paper or computer screen. Of course, there are many different types of charts, each suited to describe some situations better than others.

Choosing which chart to use in your report, proposal, or presentation should be based on two factors: the kind of information you are working with and what you are trying to say about it.

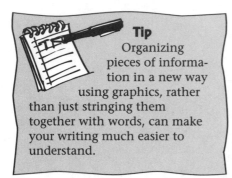

Tip
Organizing pieces of information in a new way using graphics, rather than just stringing them together with words, can make your writing much easier to understand.

You've probably heard the saying "statistics lie," which is really just suggesting that you can use numbers to support whatever point you are trying to make. Statistics can be interpreted in many ways. Depending on what you want the statistic to mean, you can probably find a way to report it so that it supports your position.

Well, the same is often true of charts. Depending on what you're trying to argue, you can select a type of chart that will make the numbers say what you want them to. You just need to know which chart will best make your point.

Tip
If you are using a spreadsheet program for your financial calculations, you can easily convert those numbers into graph form. Most software programs allow you to switch into charting mode in order to create a variety of different graphs and charts. Check the user manual for your software program to learn the specific steps.

Graphing Basics

Often graphs are used to make financial information easier to understand. Seeing a chart that shows a line representing company sales going way up suggests that things are good. And that chart probably took up a lot less space on the page than a lengthy description of the company's sales history. Visually you make the connection a lot quicker with a graph.

Different types of graphs are used depending on the following:

➤ How much information you have to present

➤ Whether you are comparing two or more sets of numbers (such as looking at this year's sales versus last year's)

➤ Whether you are dealing with raw numbers or percentages

➤ If words or numbers or both are being showcased

➤ If you are trying to illustrate a trend

Take a look at the following graphs and charts to determine which will work best for you.

Tables

Tables are square or rectangular boxes that are used to present numbers and words in an orderly fashion. Headings are listed at the top of each column, with information presented below.

There may be little or no relationship between the information in the table. For instance, if you wanted to provide a listing of recent article titles that had appeared on the subject of social security, you could create a table for easy reference. But the articles don't really have anything to do with each other. What they have in common is the subject matter: social security.

SUGGESTED READING
"Will Social Security Be There for Baby Boomers?," *Government Times*, March 1994
"How the Social Security System Works," *Business News*, June 1995
"Who Qualifies for Benefits?," *Retired Persons Newsletter*, August 1995
"The Social Security System of the Future," *Up-and-Coming Reporter*, February 1993
"Is Canada's System Better?," *Weekly Update*, April 1996
"Who's Running the Show," *Social Security Expert*, November 1994

Line Chart

A line chart is often used to show trends over time. Companies often show steady sales increases with a line chart, which gives a mini-history of how the company is doing. Each year's sales total is marked on a graph and connected by lines; hence the name "line

Tip
If your chart shows a sudden upswing, it may be referred to as a "hockey stick" because of what the line looks like.

chart." When an increase in some measure is being shown, the line in the chart is generally seen to be moving from the lower left to the upper right.

Line charts can also be used to show declines, such as a steady decrease in inventory on-hand, or sick days. In this case, the line would be moving from the upper left-hand corner of the graph down to the right.

A line chart.

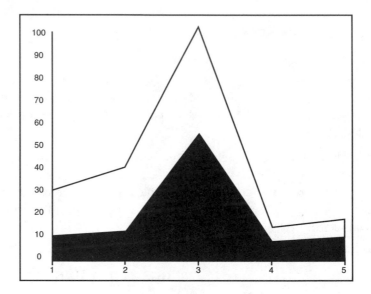

Bar Chart

Bar charts are used in the same way as line charts: to show trends falling or rising. The difference is that instead of using lines to connect dots, a solid rectangle is drawn below each point on the graph. So you end up with a series of slim bars.

Bar charts are useful when you want to compare two sets of numbers, such as last year's sales versus this year's sales for every member of your sales team. You would have two bars right next to each other for each person; one bar showing last year's sales total and one bar for this year's sales total.

While you'll generally see the bars going up and down on the chart, you may also see them used sideways. It's just a matter of personal preference as to which way you think the information looks better.

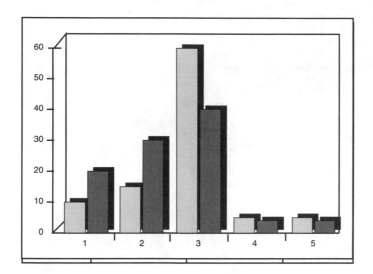

A bar chart.

Pie Chart

When you need to show how parts of a whole relate to the other pieces, you need to use a pie chart. These kinds of charts are used when you're dealing with percentages, or with numbers that can be converted to percentages.

The idea of the pie is that you can show how each piece of the pie relates to the other pieces. For example, if you wanted to report on how our tax dollars are spent, you could create a pie chart to show how big each category of spending is. Or you could design it another way, showing how much of each tax dollar is spent on certain things.

What's different about pie charts is that you need to have a total number, as well as the individual parts that make up the total in order to create one.

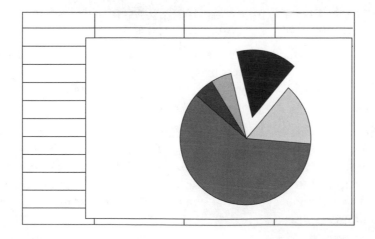

A pie chart.

117

Flow Chart

When you're trying to schedule the sections of a major project, you may find that a flow chart works best. A flow chart is a visual way to map out when things need to be done, and how they affect the other activities that need to be finished.

Flow charts are often required as part of proposal packages so that the customer can understand how you intend to complete each section of the project, and how quickly.

A flow chart.

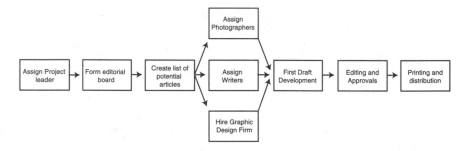

Flow Chart for the Creation of a New Customer Newsletter

Photographs Improve the Look

Many organizations can rarely afford to include photographs in their materials because the production costs are so high. Even black-and-white photos add quite a bit to the total cost. Color photos can more than double the cost to print your document.

But in some cases, a photo is the only thing that will do. Showing images of people, buildings, and situations, like the poverty of a neighborhood, can really only be portrayed effectively with a photograph.

Corporations often include photographs in annual reports that are sent out to shareholders. Proposals for multi-million dollar contracts may also feature photos. Typically, the larger the value of potential business you could win with a proposal, the more money you should be willing to invest to "wow" your prospective customer.

You'll also see that photographs are used more frequently in consumer-oriented businesses. Companies that sell to individuals, rather than to businesses, are more likely to use photos of people, products, and situations. Organizations selling to businesses may be more apt to use black-and-white photos, illustrations, or graphics. So if you're a business-to-business company, you can potentially make a big splash by incorporating color photos in your materials.

Because of the added expense, photographs are also thought to indicate how successful or aggressive a company is. The more colorful and "corporate" a company's marketing materials, for example, the more seriously they are taken in the marketplace. Photographs are often used as a measure of how well your company is doing.

That doesn't mean that photographs are always needed, or are even the best graphic to use. Illustrations are a great alternative that are less costly and often just as effective.

Illustrations Make Reading More Interesting

Illustrations, or drawings, are used when there is a story being told that cannot be complete without some visual element—and a chart just won't cut it. In many cases, illustrations are used in place of photographs because they are a lower-cost alternative.

If you have a new product being introduced, or a new building being built, having some kind of picture of what they would look like will make all the difference in the world. You can spend hours describing what a product can do for the customers, but until you show them what it looks like, they can't be totally comfortable with it. And you can't be sure that they're really getting the message. Without a visual image, people use their own imaginations to create their own version of what you described. And while creativity and imagination are good things, when you are trying to make sure customers understand your product, you don't want to leave anything to chance.

Tip
To get a sense of an illustrator's style, request to see some samples of his/her work, or set up a brief meeting to review his/her portfolio.

An Artist's Creation

Some illustrations are so impressive that they're better than photographs. The problem with photos is that they don't lie—if you have a product that looks boring, it's hard to jazz it up. Fancy lighting can make a difference, but the product still looks pretty much the same.

A trained illustrator, however, can add embellishments that make it truly beautiful. That's one major advantage of using illustrations; the results can be better than real life.

Keep in mind that the bigger the challenge the artist faces, the bigger your bill for his/her services. Drawing a picture of a scene in black-and-white is much simpler than painting it in color. And the more

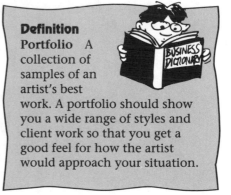

Definition
Portfolio A collection of samples of an artist's best work. A portfolio should show you a wide range of styles and client work so that you get a good feel for how the artist would approach your situation.

Definition
Bullet Point
(•) A bullet point is a dot or other mark that precedes an important phrase or sentence. Variations on the bullet point include check marks ✔, arrows ◀ ▶, and other shapes ❤.

imagination you require, the longer it takes to complete. So if it's mid-January and you want an illustrator to draw your new building as it will look in mid-July, expect to pay more.

Each illustrator is an artist with his or her own personal style. You may like the style of one illustrator and totally dislike another. To each his own. This point is important because if you decide you'd like to hire an illustrator, you're going to want to see what his/her style is before you write a check.

Illustrations can enhance your writing. (Illustrations courtesy of John MacDonald, (413) 458-0056.)

The Washington Post

Citibank

Artwork at Its Simplest

Even if you can't find an opportunity to incorporate a graph or table into your document, there are other ways to liven up your writing. For example, you can use bullet points to help highlight important sections.

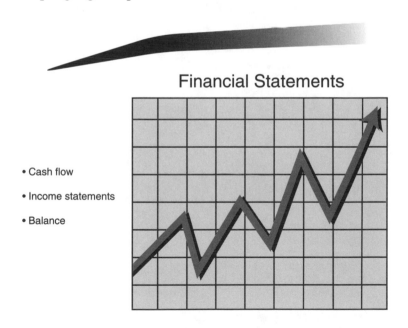

An overhead presentation using a bulleted list.

Financial Statements

• Cash flow

• Income statements

• Balance

The Least You Need to Know

➤ Graphs, charts, illustrations, and photos all help to clarify and highlight important information.

➤ There is a particular type of chart that's best for each situation.

➤ Photographs are the most expensive type of graphic to use. Illustrations are a lower-cost alternative.

➤ Bullet points (➤) have become a standard part of memos, letters, and reports as a way of identifying important sections.

Part 5
Common Types of Documents and Letters

It's one thing to learn all the rules and regulations regarding how to write and quite another thing to actually put them to use.

Now that you know how to get started in writing something, you're ready to get some specific guidance on what different types of documents look and sound like.

In this section you'll learn all about putting together letters, proposals, reports, and press materials. You'll also see actual examples of what each of these types of pieces should look like when you're done so that you're sure you've put them together correctly. Enjoy!

Chapter 15

Choosing the Appropriate Format

In This Chapter

➤ The different types of documents

➤ How to decide which format to use and when

➤ Why tone and formality often dictate format

➤ What to do if you need to respond quickly

Whether you're sending a letter, memo, proposal, or report, each type of document carries with it a certain tone or attitude. So selecting a particular type of format says a lot about how important the information is and how much it will affect your organization.

It also says something about you and how you respond to situations.

Your Options

Let's say you recently stumbled onto some information that suggested your company's advertising agency was overbilling you by falsifying their records. This is pretty hot stuff. So how do you relay this information to other people in your organization in order to determine what to do about the situation?

A *report* wouldn't be the right way to present the information because you really haven't been assigned any kind of project or investigation. A report calls for lots of supporting material—and you don't have many details to provide.

A *proposal* wouldn't be right either, because you aren't proposing anything at all. Instead, you need feedback and information from your superiors to figure out how to investigate and respond to the problem.

Since you're dealing solely with people within your organization to figure out a strategy for the situation, a *letter* really isn't appropriate. It would simply be too formal.

Definition
Email
Electronic mail. An email message is simply a typed note that is sent through your computer to someone else. In order to transmit the message, your computer must be connected to a modem.

So, it comes down to a toss-up between a memo and an email message. And the choice depends a lot on whether your company has an electronic network and how frequently people use it for sensitive information. Some companies prefer that employees only use email for internal routine correspondence about meetings and such.

So you may find that a *memo* is really the right way to go. You can send it to your boss, or whoever is in charge of managing your advertising program. Then they can distribute it to whomever they want.

Black-Tie or Casual?

When dealing with serious issues that can have negative repercussions, formality comes into play. That is, how formal do you have to be in communicating this information?

Tip
Formal documents include reports, proposals, and letters. Memos and email messages are less formal and are used primarily for internal communication only.

In this sue-happy society, we now have to be careful to report what we knew, when, and who we told in order to protect ourselves later if we or our employer get sued. So if you feel that some part of the information you are reporting could come back to haunt you, it's better to err on the side of being too formal in how you report it, rather than appear informal and unconcerned.

Evaluate each situation carefully before deciding which type of document to prepare.

What Is the Purpose?

When trying to decide which type of format to use consider why you are writing at all— what is the purpose?

To Convey Information

In many organizations, information means power. Controlling information and having access to it are serious concerns to many managers and executives, which is why many are hungry for new insights and ideas.

In many situations, you may need to communicate information simply because you have a responsibility to share it. If you've done some research, investigated something at the request of your boss, or simply thought of a new idea that could benefit others, you'll want to write it down and distribute it.

You may also need to express an opinion or relate an experience you've had (especially if it was bad) to a vendor, customer, or colleague.

To Ask for Guidance

Instead of being an information source, sometimes you need to seek out a resource. Many times we all need to locate some new information, ask for advice, get some feedback from an outsider, or just gather new information. Asking for help, or information, is another reason to correspond with someone.

To Suggest Something New

Suggesting a new approach, or asking for approval to proceed with some action is a third reason for preparing a business document. Customers may ask you to consider how to complete something for them, or you may see an opportunity you want to pursue on your own.

Who Will See It?

An organization's hierarchy or reporting structure also affects what type of document to prepare.

Management

Will people above you, such as your boss, be reviewing the information you put together? And will people above him/her see it? How far up will this information be passed, potentially? Gauging this is important.

Peers

On the other hand, if people who work with you are the intended audience, you'd write something totally different, wouldn't you? The tone, length, and style would be much less formal than if management were going to review it.

A Group or an Individual?

Whether you're communicating to an individual or to several people impacts how you might write up your information. You actually have more options for communicating with individuals than when dealing with groups of people. For example, it's easier to call one person than take the time to type a note. However, it's more efficient to send a memo to a group of people.

Internal or External?

When deciding what type of document to prepare, determining who will ultimately see it is an important consideration. Some types of documents are designed for use within an organization and are less formal than those designed to go outside the organization.

Employees and Staff Members

People who report to you, or whom you work with, require less formal communication than people whom you report to. When providing information to people you work with, memos and email are the standard way to go. They're quick, easy, and not too complicated (unless you're computer illiterate, and then it may take some time to figure out that electronic mail system).

Tip
There's no need to type up pages and pages of information when you're dealing with an internal request, but prepare a scaled-down version of a proposal within your memo or letter.

You may also use a memo when providing information to your boss or other higher-ups. But when you're trying to get approval for a new project, for new funding, or for a new employee, consider using more of a proposal-type format.

Some situations require more background information on why you need something. For example, if you want to hire an administrative assistant, you will need to explain what this request will cost the company and how it will benefit the company as well. In effect, you're *proposing* a new hire.

Customers, Prospects, and Suppliers

People outside your organization require more formality than those within. So you will rarely write a memo to a customer or supplier. In some cases, such as if your company has formed an alliance or partnership with a supplier, it may be okay to use a memo because they are almost considered part of the company.

In most cases, you'll use letters for short messages and correspondence, proposals to try to get new business from existing or new customers, and reports to relay important observations or progress updates to customers and suppliers.

If you're not sure which format to use, keep in mind that it's always better to err on the side of being a little too formal.

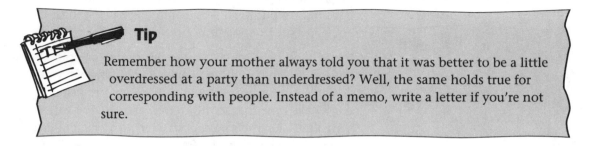

Tip

Remember how your mother always told you that it was better to be a little overdressed at a party than underdressed? Well, the same holds true for corresponding with people. Instead of a memo, write a letter if you're not sure.

How Quickly Do You Need a Response?

The urgency of getting a response is an important element in figuring out the best way to communicate with someone. You must also consider how quickly you need to respond to someone else's request for information.

Get Back to Me As Soon As Possible

Although we're focusing on how to use written documents to improve communication, sometimes there's just no substitute for the telephone. Granted, there are drawbacks. For one, you have no written record of what was said in case there is confusion or disagreement later. It is also often difficult or time-consuming to review information that could be more easily conveyed on paper. But what it lacks in permanency, the telephone makes up for in timeliness.

You Need to Reply Immediately

If you've been asked to get back to someone with information right away, and the information is not very complicated, it's once again best to place a phone call. For instance, if your boss is trying to set up a three-way conference call and wants to know if you're free on Monday at 3:00 pm, just pick up the phone. There's no reason to spend the time typing up a memo to confirm that you're available.

Another device you should consider is the fax machine. Let's say you have to alert a group of customers of a special deal your company is offering on a particular product line. The advantage of faxing this message is that it will get out just as quickly as a phone call. And you'll have a written record to fall back on if there's ever any question about what the offer was. What is even better is that you can have an assistant operate the fax machine so that you're working on other tasks while your message is being distributed.

In some cases, however, you'll need to relay complicated information in a timely fashion. For instance, let's say a customer calls you at 4:00 p.m. requesting that he receives information from you by tomorrow. Well, you know right off the bat that you simply don't have time to put together a comprehensive proposal. There just aren't enough hours in the day.

Tip

First consider how much time you've been given to prepare a response to a request for information. Then estimate how much time it will take you to respond. And, finally, determine what format should be used given your time constraints.

If you don't have much time to respond to a request, your options for what you can provide in the way of written documents is severely limited. For example, since you don't have time to respond to the case described above with a full-blown proposal, consider writing a one-page quote or a proposal in the form of a multi-paged letter.

On the other hand, if you have several weeks to prepare, you should be able to write up a winning proposal that covers every major issue. While we've used a proposal as an example here, the same guidelines hold true for letters, reports, and memos.

The Least You Need to Know

➤ When choosing which document to use, take into consideration the tone and level of formality needed.

➤ Consider why you are writing at all—the purpose of your document.

➤ Also consider who will see the information you're preparing. Will it be your boss or your peers?

➤ Evaluate the urgency of a response. Sometimes a short document or a simple telephone call is best.

➤ Don't take any chances; it's better to be a little too formal than appear informal and unconcerned.

Memos

Memos are the typical corporate communiquè. Everyone gets them. Everyone sends them. And they're one of the easiest types of documents to put together. They're also one of the shortest.

Frequently one page or less in length, memos are not detailed documents. They are often used to bring up issues, ask questions, and respond to questions others have posed in earlier memos.

When Do I Use One?

In its simplest form, a memo is a note to someone you work with which provides information they need or asks a question that you need answered. The format is simple and the length is short, which is probably why everyone prefers sending a memo to sending a letter.

Memos are generally used only for communication among employees within an organization. They are not used to communicate with people who are not employed by the same company. However, in this new age of partnerships and collaborative projects, some of those boundaries are being blurred and a memo may be permitted to go "outside" to a supplier or vendor.

What's the Point?

A memo conveys information about a particular subject to someone, or to a group of someones, in your organization. In general, memos are devoted to a single subject. This is so that it is easy for people to respond quickly. Thinking about and answering a single question is a heck of a lot easier than having to come up with information related to several issues.

Let's say, for instance, you've been asked to gather a total of eight documents. You've found five of them in your filing cabinets, but you can't find the other three documents. What do you do? Do you send back the information incomplete or do you hold on to the whole package until you can get everything together? Most people tend to hold on to the request until they can respond thoroughly, which slows up the process.

Warning
Criticizing or reprimanding someone is better done in private, or in a note to that person alone.

Memos should only address one or two subjects at one time. Of course, this may mean that you have to write twice as many memos to cover all the information you need. This is probably why you see so many memos floating around.

Watch What You Say

Since memos are often sent to several people at once, they are very public documents; so you probably don't want to use a memo to give a tongue lashing.

If your memo contains something you don't want revealed to everyone, it should be stamped "business confidential" or "internal use only," or say somewhere within the memo that the information shouldn't be released. Remember, the primary purpose of a memo is to share information.

When to Send One

Situations in which you would send a memo include:

➤ To provide minutes of a meeting recently held

➤ To announce a meeting that has been scheduled

➤ To set an agenda for an upcoming meeting

➤ To request some action

➤ To respond to a memo received

➤ To summarize or report on a decision made

➤ To provide an update on an ongoing situation

➤ To provide new information or make an announcement

➤ To be used as a cover for distributing materials

Providing Minutes of a Meeting Recently Held

Meeting minutes are just one form of a memo, written for the purpose of keeping everyone on a committee, project team, or board of directors abreast of what's going on.

When someone is appointed secretary or scribe for a meeting, it is his responsibility to take notes on what was discussed and decided at the meeting. He also needs to distribute a summary to everyone who was in attendance. Meeting minutes are even more important to people who missed the meeting and want to be kept up-to-date on what happened.

Since everyone receiving the minutes knows why they are getting them, any kind of introduction or explanation is unnecessary. So the memo should start right off with a description of what was discussed first, what some of the issues and concerns were, and what was decided.

Tip
The people to include on the memo's cc: list are the people who were invited to the meeting.

Announcing That a Meeting Has Been Scheduled

In addition to reporting on what happened in the recent past at a meeting, a memo is the best way to announce an upcoming meeting and alert everyone that they should put it on their calendars.

You can also use a memo to ask people whether they are available to meet on a certain date at a certain time. State what the potential times are for the meeting and ask them to get back to you with their schedules. You can then schedule the next meeting based on everyone's availability.

Setting an Agenda for an Upcoming Meeting

Meetings can be such a waste of time if the wrong people are there, or if the right people are there and they don't know what they need to be doing.

To make the most of every meeting, issue a memo prior to the next meeting that lists the proposed discussion topics. Written in the form of a meeting agenda, the memo helps to get everyone thinking about important issues and how they think the group should address them.

Requests for Some Action

Sometimes picking up the phone and asking for something is the easiest way to get it taken care of. However, when you're tackling a major project and need several people to provide information, it's easier to send a memo to everyone identifying what you need and when you need it done.

Sending a written request also helps you stay on top of things because you can add the memo to your project file or tickler to remind you of what you asked for.

Definition

Tickler   A type of file that consists of 31 days and 12 months, so you can put a note or reminder in a specific future month or daily file to remind you to do something. It's a very helpful follow-up system.

Response to a Memo Received

The best response to a memo asking for information is in the form of a memo providing what was requested. Busy people appreciate receiving written confirmation and information because verbal messages often get garbled or misplaced. It's safer in most instances to respond to a memo by typing up your own.

Summary or Report on a Decision Made

When an issue has been decided or a decision made that is of interest to a group of people, it's best to prepare a memo reporting on the results. That way, everyone gets the same information at the same time. Otherwise, someone may feel left out of the loop if they heard the information last.

And in many cases, if the information is somewhat lengthy or involved, it helps to have a written document to refer to. Sometimes that helps in understanding what has happened.

Provide an Update on an Ongoing Situation

Progress reports to your boss, or to a committee, are one type of memo. These reports are simply updates that keep everyone informed regarding what's going on.

Used as a Cover for Distributing Materials

When you send out new marketing materials to the salesforce, or provide updated insurance information to all employees, it's smart to attach a memo up-front to tell them about what they're receiving. To just send out some new information without an explanation is dangerous. Not only will people not understand what they're getting: they won't know why it was sent. A cover memo clears up the confusion.

Provide New Information or Make an Announcement

Memos are great for making announcements. Whenever there is new information to impart or some kind of announcement to be made, a memo allows you to put the details in black-and-white and send it out to large groups of people. In situations where many people need to receive the announcement, a memo can be extremely efficient.

Memo Dos and Don'ts

Since memos are such simple documents, there aren't that many rules on how to use them. However, there are a few dos and don'ts to be aware of:

Dos

➤ Do carbon copy others within your organization who need to see your memo, such as members of a project team or employees in your department.

➤ Do send a memo to people who report directly to you and let them distribute it within their departments or divisions as they see fit.

➤ Do use bullet points and other graphics to identify the key points or issues you're addressing.

➤ Do stamp sensitive memos with "business confidential" or "for internal use only" to inform people not to let anyone else know what they've just been told.

Definition
Carbon Copy This means that you'll send copies of the same memo to other people. Others who will receive a copy are listed after the "cc:" symbol, which stands for carbon copy.

Don'ts

➤ Don't cover too many issues in one memo. It's better to have a single memo address a single topic.

➤ Don't cc: everyone and their brother. Determine who really needs this information and leave it at that.

➤ Don't send a memo to anyone higher up than your immediate supervisor. Let your boss decide who above her should also see it.

➤ Don't send memos to customers or prospects. A letter is better.

➤ Don't use a memo to correct wayward employees or identify weaknesses they need to work on. A personal note or a private discussion is better. A memo is too informal for such messages.

What Should It Look Like?

The standard memo format is amazingly simple, but keep in mind that organizations often create their own form. You may notice that company memos have a certain "look" that is slightly different from the standard memo presented here.

Date:
To:
From:
Subject:

Body of memo

➤ Left justified

➤ A space between paragraphs

➤ Single space

Carbon copy

The standard memo.

Tip

The basic layout has information regarding who is sending the memo and who is receiving it at the top of the page. The rest of the page is for reporting whatever there is to report. Slight modifications in the placement of the items at the top of the page are permitted.

Variations that your company may choose that don't affect the layout include:

➤ Bolding the Date, To, From, and Subject elements for emphasis.

➤ Adding a horizontal line below the Subject line to mark off the beginning of the memo.

➤ Moving the Carbon Copy notation to underneath the "From" line.

Samples

M E M O

TO: Joe Bennett
           Mary Cohen
           Cheryl Flanagan
           Donna Simpson

FROM: Kathy West

DATE: December 20, 1996

RE: Training budget for 1997

We have just completed the budgeting process for next year and have established several key areas to focus on. One of those areas is skill-building.

In order to continue to improve the quality of our products and the abilities of our employees, we have decided to invest $4,000 per employee on training during 1997.

During the month of January, I will meet with each of you individually to set goals, review your current skill level in a variety of areas, and to start to identify potential training sessions you should attend.

Please stop by my office sometime next week and pick up an assessment form that we'll go over in our meeting.

If you have any questions, please call me.

MEMORANDUM

DATE: April 30, 1995

TO: Human Resource department

FROM: Ann Shannon

RE: Summer hours

As we have in past years, the company will switch to summer hours as of the day after Memorial Day.

This means that Monday through Thursday we will work from 7:30 am to 5:00 pm and from 7:30 am to 12:00 pm on Fridays. We hope that this will allow everyone to enjoy longer weekends.

Regular hours will resume the day after Labor Day.

If you have any questions, please call me at extension 123.

The Least You Need to Know

➤ Memos are used to distribute information within an organization.

➤ Most memos are one page, or less, in length.

➤ Limit the number of major topics addressed in a memo to one.

➤ The format for a memo includes a line for the date, who you're sending it to, who you are, and what it's about.

Chapter 17

Email
Messages

In This Chapter

➤ What's email and how do you use it?

➤ Email vs. typed memos

➤ How to get hooked—intracompany email and commercial services

➤ Email etiquette

Just a few short years ago, there were only a handful of options available to get a message to someone; by telephone; by mail; and by telegram. Then fascsimile machines, overnight mail services like FedEx and Airborne Express, and the most recent craze, electronic mail, all appeared on the market.

Of all the means of communication just listed, electronic mail—generally referred to as "email"—is the fastest and the least expensive way to get your messages to someone. Which is why you should definitely become more familiar with how to use it.

What Is Email?

An email message is simply a typed note that is sent through your computer to someone else. In order to transmit the message, your computer must be connected to a modem.

Definition

Modem   A small device that links your computer to telephone lines, which carry your email messages to other computers hooked up to a modem. You can buy a computer with an "internal modem," or you can purchase an "external modem" that just plugs into your computer and a phone jack.

While anyone with a computer and modem can potentially send messages electronically to someone else, there are two different types of electronic mail systems to be aware of: intracompany and commercial.

Intracompany Email

Many larger corporations and universities have computer networks installed to allow employees or students and faculty members to send messages to each other. All the computers in the organization can be linked together using cables and software programs, so that they can talk to each other. In this case, modems aren't needed because the computers are all connected through the cabling.

Kodak employees, for instance, use a program called PROFS to send email to other Kodakers, and the University of Pennsylvania has PennNet to link students, faculty, and staff to each other via computer.

Besides sending messages, you can do other things through the network, too, such as keeping a daily schedule of your appointments, scanning a listing of upcoming training programs, and searching various company databases.

Some corporations prefer to set up their own internal communications network because messages being shared among employees can't be easily read by outsiders. This also means that employees will find it difficult to send messages to people outside of the company who aren't on the internal network.

This doesn't mean you can't send email to people outside your organization—people do it all the time—it just means you may need to use a commercial service to do it.

Commercial Services

There are computer services now available called online services that allow anyone with a computer, a modem, and a credit card (for billing) to send and receive messages from anywhere in the world.

Definition

Online Service A computer network that has been set up by a for-profit company to allow users to send and receive email messages, and search for information such as recent magazine articles, stock performance, or the weather in Aruba (sunny, sunny, sunny). The biggest online services are America Online, CompuServe, and Prodigy.

Tip

To try out one of the online services, call them and ask for a free trial package. The three major services can be reached at these toll free numbers:

America Online: 800-827-6364

CompuServe: 800-554-4079

Prodigy: 800-776-3449

You will receive software that allows you to use the service free for a few hours (each company's offer is different). After the free trial ends, however, you'll pay a fee based on how much you use it.

The Internet is another network that permits email communication. It is set up differently from the commercial services in that it was created by the government (in the 1960s), so it isn't owned or run by a single company as the other commercial services are.

You can send and receive email messages from other people who are on the Internet, as well as check out information on the World Wide Web, which is a huge promotional section with information on different companies and products. It also features interesting tidbits and cross-references to other areas of related information.

Tip

To take a look at what's on the Internet, look in your local Yellow Page directory for a listing of Internet Access Providers. (Some directories may still list them under "Computers.") Give them a call to find out their monthly fees. The costs can vary widely, so call several for prices.

What's So Great About It?

Email is beating typed memos and voice mail in terms of popularity for several reasons:

➤ **High-tech appeal**   Sending email shows that you're up on the latest technological trends, and that you have a computer on your desk. Heck, anyone can send a typed memo, but it's a more elite group that has the capability to send electronic messages.

➤ **Immediate gratification**   Messages are sent virtually instantaneously to the recipient. Although we used to think that overnight services were the fastest thing around, email is now even faster.

➤ **Inexpensive**   If you send a message through an internal company system, chances are that there is no cost to you at all. And even if you use a commercial online service, the most you would pay for a single message is around 15¢. That's still cheaper than a letter mailed first class, or a long distance fax.

➤ **Environmentally friendly**   The only resource email messages use is electricity; no paper is needed. So think about all the paper you're saving by not mailing out a memo to 50 people.

➤ **Backup evidence**   While email messages aren't sent on paper, you can always choose to print out and file away certain sensitive messages that could prove useful later.

Tip
When someone asks you to send them something using "snail mail," they want you to send it via the U.S. Postal Service.

➤ **Versatility**   Messages can be sent to any amount of individuals. For example, you can send an e-mail just to your boss to confirm a meeting for tomorrow or you can send an e-mail to a long list of people who may be on a committee you're heading.

➤ **Brevity**   Though you may be tempted to try and fill up an 8 1/2 × 11 sheet of paper with additional information just so it looks more impressive, the advantage of email is that short messages are generally preferred to long ones. So you'll save time, too.

Sending Documents and Files

Although most email messages are short notes between people, you should also be aware that whole files can be sent as a message. If you've already typed a memo using your word processing software and don't want to retype it into an email message, you can just send the whole file containing your memo. Most systems have a "send file" command that asks you which file you want to send and to whom you want it sent. Once you tell the computer to transmit it, the file appears in the other person's mailbox.

Sending whole files electronically saves you the hassle of printing out documents and mailing or faxing them to the intended recipient. Another advantage of sending the file is that the other person can open the file using his own software, make any needed changes or corrections on his computer, and then send it back to you electronically if need be. Editing online saves both time and money.

Email Dos and Don'ts

To make sure you don't irritate someone, follow these simple online rules of etiquette:

Dos

➤ Do keep messages short. People are getting more and more email and want to be able to get through their messages quickly. Unless someone specifically asked you to send them a lengthy document or file, stick to short notes.

➤ Do check your email messages frequently. The biggest appeal of email is its immediacy; people don't like to wait days to hear back from you. So go into your email mailbox at least daily (some people check hourly) to get your messages and ensure you can respond quickly.

Don'ts

➤ Don't send politically sensitive messages via email. Use caution when using email to forward bad news or information you wouldn't want made public. Once you've sent a message it can be printed out by the recipient and used against you later or, worse, a talented programmer can find the message on the system and publicize the information.

➤ Don't get too informal. Although the tendency is to write less formally than in an official memo, if you are sending a message to a client, an associate, or your boss, be just as professional as you would in a typical memo or letter you'd send her.

➤ Don't send personal messages if you're on an internal company network. Although everyone has done it at one point or another, be careful about what you say in your messages. You never know who could accidentally get a private message meant for you, or vice versa.

➤ Don't use email to avoid phone conversations. Email is convenient because it allows you to send people a message at your convenience and they can pick it up at their convenience. But if you never pick up the phone to speak directly to someone, you could give the message that you're avoiding them. Personal contact from time to time is necessary to solidify business and personal relationships, so don't give up on phone calls and letters.

➤ Don't type using all caps in your messages. When the computer was first intro-duced, I remember that the printer could only print using capital letters; there were no lower case fonts. But nowadays, there is no reason to type using all caps unless you want to emphasize a particular word or point. If you type your whole message using only capital letters, people reading your message will think that you are screaming at them.

➤ Don't overuse "smileys" or acronyms. Although smileys and acronyms help to facilitate communication and cut down on typing lengthy phrases, be careful not to rely too heavily on them. A memo decorated with smiley symbols at every turn will not be taken too seriously, no matter what the content of the message is. And acronyms can be irritating to people who aren't familiar with them.

Definition

Smileys Symbols used in electronic communication to help replace facial gestures you normally see when talking directly to someone. They help communicate someone's mood, or indicate when someone's joking. The most typical smiley is :), which, if you tilt your head to the left, is two eyes and a smiling face. Following are other common smileys and their meanings:

:-)	Smile
;-)	Wink
:-(	Frown
:-D	Laugh
:-X	No comment

Frequently used acronyms are:

MSG Message

JIC Just in case

CUL See you later

FAQ   Frequently asked question

IMHO   In my humble opinion

BTW   By the way

<g>   Grin

<vbg>   Very big grin

And my personal favorite, **TTFN**   Ta ta for now

Writing an Eye-Catching Subject Line

Email messages are written a lot like memos, with the person you're sending the message to listed at the top, along with your name or identifier, and a subject line. In memos, the subject line serves to alert the reader to the topic of the memo. In email, they serve the same purpose but they're even more important.

If you have an email account, you're probably deluged with mail every day. Some messages are from people you may not even know. Or worse, they're junk mail. Your subject line helps weed out the junk messages from the important ones.

To make your email message one of the first to be read, type a short heading that has impact and makes the reader want to immediately open it. Try and summarize the most important point in your message in a few words and use that as your subject line.

For instance, if your email is about getting expense reports in by a certain day, the subject line you type might be "Expense reports due" or "Don't Miss this Date." Unfortunately, you can't get too creative or your message will start to look like those junk mail letters offering "FREE MONEY" or "Save Hundreds on Your Phone Bill."

Keep in mind that your subject line can only accept a certain number of letters and spaces, or characters. So it needs to be short and sweet. And it needs to make sense. Put the essence of your message in your subject line to be sure it gets noticed, and read promptly.

What Should an Email Message Look Like?

Most electronic mail programs don't allow much leeway in formatting. To send a message you need to know the recipient's name and electronic mail address. Underneath those two pieces of information is generally a subject line where you can indicate what your message is about. You can start typing your note below the subject line, starting a new paragraph when needed.

Most organizations have a standard "look" to their documents that you can follow when creating a memo or message, such as the type of font that is preferred, the size of the margins, whether the document is left justified or centered, and so on. But with email there is usually just one font available and little you can do in the way of formatting. So don't get bogged down trying to make it look pretty when it's just not necessary.

Examples

Here are some typical email messages to give you an idea of what they should look and sound like:

```
From:  Marcia Layton, 71045,2627
To:  David Smith, 72204,6262
Date:  Wed, May 15, 1996, 6:05 PM
RE:  Client meeting

Our meeting with Jane Grant has been postponed until next Tuesday
because of a scheduling conflict. I'll get back to you with a new day
and time when I hear from her.

Marcia
```

```
From:  Marcia Layton, 71045,2627
To:  Marj Crum, 76032,2656
Date:  Wed, May 15, 1996, 6:12 PM
RE:  Starboard Media Group

Hi Marj,
I'm working with a client who needs to develop some top-notch market-
ing materials in a rather short timeframe. Could you give me a quote
to design the following pieces of literature:

4-page, 4-color marketing brochure
2-page, 2-color sell sheet
Pocket folder with logo on front
Letterhead, business card, envelope

He's looking to get started in the next couple of weeks.

Thanks for your help.

Marcia
```

The Least You Need to Know

➤ There are two ways to send email—through an internal company network or through a commercial service.

➤ Email can consist of short messages or entire files.

➤ Keep your email messages brief and professional at all times.

➤ Don't overuse acronyms and symbols.

➤ Never type IN ALL CAPS when sending a message; it implies that you are screaming at the recipient.

Business Letters

Letters have got to be the most frequently used form of communication in business. There are so many reasons to send letters, and so many people to send them to.

Although memos are generally used for communication within an organization, letters are used to convey information to people outside. For example, you would never send a memo to a potential customer, or to a job candidate. You'd send a letter. A letter adds just a touch of formality that is expected when two colleagues, associates, or business partners exchange information.

Tip
Your business letter should convey a positive and upbeat attitude that will make people want to do business with you.

The Standard Format

In personal letter writing, the emphasis is on the story and on strengthening the relationship you have with the other person. However, with business letters, professionalism is the key. Unlike a memo, which has no introduction or lead-in, a letter has a beginning, middle, and an end. We'll go through specific formatting information later in this chapter, but for now, familiarize yourself with the different parts of a letter:

The basic parts of a letter.

LAYTON&CO.

```
Your name and return address
Today's date
Your contact's name and address




Salutation (Dear Mr./Ms.)

The body of the letter
```

```
The close (Yours truly/Sincerely yours/Regards)
Your signature
Your typed name and title

Carbon copy notation (cc:)

Postscript (P.S.)

Enclosure
```

The Introduction

The introduction of your letter can consist of one paragraph or several paragraphs that clearly explain the purpose of your letter—why you are writing. People often get frustrated when they receive vague letters that meander all over the place and never really explain why the person bothered writing it in the first place. Those types of letters are a waste of time for everyone involved.

Telling your readers right away why you are writing also helps them determine how to act on your letter—should they forward it to someone else in their organization who is in a better position to respond, should they file it away for future action, or should they make copies and send it out to everyone in the company?

If you are writing to complain to a manufacturer about a defective car you just bought, for instance, you need to state right off the bat that your car has unrepairable problems:

> Dear Mr. Jones,
>
> I recently purchased a new 1996 Autolux car that has had a series of problems since I drove it off the lot. I have spoken with the local dealer, who has been unable to repair the car, and he suggested that I write to you directly to try to determine what should be done about the car.

Or perhaps you are writing a letter of appreciation to a supplier. You might start off with:

> Dear Ms. Smith,
>
> Your print production team is amazing. Last week they went above and beyond the call of duty to help us out with our new flyer, and I wanted to write and tell you how great a job they are doing.

As you can see, the introduction sets up the rest of the letter, which consists of the body and the close.

The Body

Now that you've explained the point of your letter, you need to provide supporting evidence to further explain yourself. For example, if you are writing to request information on a company's product line, you might state the specific type of information you are interested in (a brochure? video? technical manual?), why you want it (you are considering buying one in the next 6 months or you're thinking about upgrading to this new model), and any particular questions you have about the product.

Or, if you are writing a letter about offering someone a new job, you would lead off by congratulating her on being offered this great new job. Then in the body of the letter you should describe the specifics of what you are offering. This might include the salary, vacation time, benefits, dress code, responsibilities of the position, reporting structure, and anything else that would be of immediate interest to your applicant.

If you are writing a complaint letter, you need to provide specifics that clearly explain why you're complaining. Does your bicycle have faulty brakes? Are the pages in your book falling out? Just saying that there is a problem doesn't help your reader determine a way to correct the situation.

Let's say you've decided to write a complaint letter to your local copy shop after your order was lost for the third time in the same week. To show that the store manager has a continuing problem on his hands, mention any previous problems you also experienced with the shop. Try to describe specific instances so that the store manager can pinpoint where the problems are occurring.

Remember, when faced with a complaint, most people look for a way to fix the situation and make you feel better. Your objective, therefore, should be to clearly explain why you're upset and to help the recipient of the letter find a way to rectify the situation to your satisfaction.

The Close

The end of your letter should summarize the points you made in the introduction and in the body and suggest what your next step should be. Remember, a letter is only successful if the person receiving it understands why you wrote it and what, if anything, he is expected to do next. For example, if you are writing a sales letter and intend to follow up on it, you might want to say the following in your last paragraph: "I'll call you next week to inquire about the possibility of a meeting to discuss my proposal."

Or if you need a job candidate to make a decision by a certain date, you might want to say: "We're eager to have a new vice president of marketing in place by early next month, so I would appreciate it if you would get back to me with your answer by next Friday, April 16th."

If you are complaining about your erratic car, you may request to receive a new one under the lemon law, or you may just want the problem to be fixed at no cost to you. Whatever your request is, close your letter by stating exactly what you want done and how you intend to further contact the person.

Sometimes there is no reason for the recipient to respond, as in the case of thank you letters. However, the reader should be able to recognize the letter for what it is—an expression of gratitude.

Reasons to Write One

In general, you write a business letter to report good news, bad news, or to make a request. Although you may write personal letters just to keep in touch with friends and family, all business letters (good or bad) must always have a purpose.

Good News

Responding to or providing good news to someone is one reason for a letter. Although the telephone is now used frequently in place of a letter, people still enjoy receiving a piece of paper that they can hold on to.

When there is good news to be shared such as a job offer, recognition for a job well done, or a congratulations for winning the lottery (no, I've never received one), the tangible document that the news arrives on is often saved. Have you ever noticed framed letters of praise or thanks in a person's office? Those letters are valuable because they serve as proof that the recipient is a hard worker, a dedicated volunteer, or a talented performer.

Whenever you have the chance to share good news with someone, don't just make a phone call; put it in writing so it can be shown off.

Cover Letter

Cover letters are short letters sent to accompany something else such as a brochure, application, or résumé. In many instances, the cover letter is inserted simply to explain what is being enclosed. For example, if you have been asked by a potential customer to mail him a sample of your company's product, you wouldn't just drop the sample in the mail without some sort of note.

Always consider the person on the receiving end of your mail. When she opens the envelope or box, is she going to know who sent it and why? Will she know what to do next? This should all be explained in the cover letter.

Fundraising Letter

If you work for a non-profit organization, a school or college, or a community group, you may find that you are constantly writing to people to ask for money. In any situation where you are working to raise money or gather support for a cause, you are trying to persuade someone to do something for you. These types of persuasive letters frequently rely on:

➤ Empathy—Trying to get readers to relate to the people who will benefit from their donation, pledge, or assistance.

➤ Hope—Explaining how donations will help people in the long run.

➤ Guilt—Making people feel that your request is needed and is a reasonable one that will hardly drain their wallets.

Request Letter

After seeing an advertisement for free information on a new business opportunity, you may want to request that a packet be sent to you. When writing a request letter, make sure to keep it short and simple and clearly explain what you want and why. For example, you may write that you're requesting to receive the information listed in the March 12 ad in *Newsweek*.

Thank You Letter

Studies have shown time and time again that what employees appreciate most is recognition for a job well done. Your letter of thanks doesn't have to be lengthy since you're just focusing on what the person did to help you.

When writing a thank you letter, first consider who you are going to send it to. If you want to express appreciation to an employee, address the letter to that person's boss with a carbon copy to the individual. You are then not only thanking the person for a job well done, but you are telling the company what a great employee that person is. Thank you notes are so important at some department stores that they are counted when someone is being considered for a raise or promotion. So you can actually affect whether someone gets a good raise by just taking a few minutes to say "thanks."

Acknowledgement Letter

It is always good practice to send a letter to someone acknowledging that you received that person's letter. For example, if a customer placed an order with you, you should send him an acknowledgement letter reassuring him that you received his order and that it is being processed. You should also take the opportunity to thank the customer for ordering from you.

Many corporations receive résumés on a daily basis from would-be employees. Although it is simply impossible to follow up on every application, a letter should be sent to each individual letting him know that his résumé was received and that it is being evaluated.

In some cases, you may receive a letter that requires some action on your part that could take some time. For instance, customers may write to report on some faulty information they received and that they want you to know about. In such cases, it is better to send an acknowledgement letter out right away so that the senders know that you're aware of the problem and that you're looking into it. Sending the acknowledgement letter out first will prevent you from being hounded by phone calls later.

Bad News

Good news letters are fun to write because you know that you're going to make the person receiving it feel good. Bad news letters, on the other hand, are not enjoyable to write since they can make someone feel disappointed, sad, angry, or frustrated. However, you can lessen the pain caused by the bad news just in the way you write your letter.

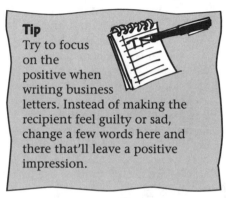

Tip
Try to focus on the positive when writing business letters. Instead of making the recipient feel guilty or sad, change a few words here and there that'll leave a positive impression.

To begin with, start your letter with some good news. For example, you may begin with a sincere compliment about the recipient: "You did a wonderful job last month on the company's newsletter," or "You've always been reliable." Then state whatever the bad news is as quickly as possible. Finally, finish the letter with an encouraging message. Below are a few typical bad news letters that you may be called on to write from time to time.

Problem Letter

There are two kinds of problem letters. The first one is about a problem that you have experienced. The second one is about a problem you know that your customer is about to experience.

1. You have a problem. Let's say you've just bought a new clothes dryer, had it installed, and now find that it doesn't dry your clothes completely. You probably want your problem resolved right away. So after trying to work things out with your local appliance dealer who sold you the dryer, you may find that you have to appeal directly to the manufacturer with a letter.

To push someone else to help you with a problem, you need to first help them understand what your problem is. In this case, you've purchased a new dryer and it is defective. You've also attempted to fix the problem by contacting the retailer who sold it to you and have gotten nowhere. Therefore, the reason you are writing the letter is to request that the manufacturer step in and help you. Now you have to decide what they can do to help fix the problem for you. Do you want a new dryer? Do you want your money refunded so you can buy a different dryer? Do you want this one repaired?

2. Your customer is going to have a problem. What's worse than having to write to someone about how you screwed up. However, sometimes you have to be the bearer of bad news. For example, if a shipment has been delayed and now your customers are not going to get their orders on time, that's bad news that has to be conveyed.

When breaking bad news to someone, it's best to start off with an expression of appreciation or good news. In this case, you'd want to thank your customers for their orders.

Tip
Make sure that you're not one of those negative people who are constantly complaining about something. Instead, try to always look for and communicate the potential positives of every situation. Complainers tend to make enemies fast and rarely get what they want. Ask nicely, however, and you're likely to succeed.

Next, you'll need to tell them that their order is going to be delayed until such-and-such date because your supplier was late in their delivery. Be as specific as possible about when the problem will be resolved. If you know when the new arrival date is for the merchandise, tell your customers exactly when they can expect to receive their orders.

And to make them feel better about the whole situation, you might close your letter by offering some sort of thank you gift for their understanding and patience (a gift certificate towards their next order, for example). You also might give them some control over the whole situation by offering them the option of cancelling their order or exchanging it for something else they can receive right away.

Demonstrating to your customers that you are trying to bend over backward to please them will reduce their anger toward you for inconveniencing them. Hopefully, they will also appreciate everything you are trying to do to fix their problem.

Denial Letter

Generally when you deny someone something, you are giving them bad news. So to make them feel better, just as before, you should start and end your letter with a positive statement. Whatever you are denying should be mentioned only in the body of the letter.

A denial letter might be used to send to job applicants who submitted résumés but didn't get the job. It could also be sent to someone who applied for a store credit card but wasn't approved and to a customer who requested a refund of a non-refundable deposit.

Complaint Letter

Although you may want to try to speak to someone by phone first to see if you can get a matter cleared up, in many cases, you'll need to put your complaint in writing first before you'll get action.

Like all bad news letters, you should start off your complaint letter with something nice to say. If you're having a problem with a customer service representative at one of your suppliers, you can still start your letter by telling the president how much you have always enjoyed working with the company. Or if this is a new relationship, tell him how much you were looking forward to establishing a long-term business relationship. If you have to, refer back to how well things have gone in the past. Anything to find a positive way to start your letter.

Then shift to stating clearly what the problem is that needs to be fixed. Follow up your initial description of the problem with as much detail as you can about how the problem came about and what you've done to try and correct the situation. Don't be nasty or overly critical; just state what isn't going right and what you've done so far to rectify it.

Finally, tell the reader what you'd like done. How do you think the problem can be corrected in a way that both of you will be happy? If you don't have any ideas in this regard, then just suggest that you get together to discuss resolving the matter. At least you've explained that there is a problem and that things need to change.

Then close the letter with a positive statement about the future, saying something to the effect that you're confident everything can be worked out.

Collection/Billing

Asking customers to pay their bills is awkward at times. You want to be paid, but you don't want to damage a good relationship with your clients. Therefore, a brief note explaining that you previously submitted an invoice and have not yet received a payment is all that is needed as a first reminder. It lets your customers know that you have been patient, but that they should now pay their bill.

If this note is ignored, you need to get a little more forceful—but never rude or critical. Explain in your second letter that their payment is overdue and that you would appreciate their sending the check immediately. Depending on how long it has been since you sent the first invoice (when it gets past 60 days you should start to be concerned), you may want to mention that if they don't respond, you'll be forced to begin collection proceedings. Of course, "collection proceedings" is a fairly vague term that can mean anything from filing a small claims suit to putting their past due invoice into a different file folder. That's up to you.

> **Tip**
> Customers and colleagues who are constantly pessimistic and always looking for something to go wrong are not people you want to be around. They're also not people you want to do business with. Who needs the added stress of dealing with someone who will leave you feeling down?! You certainly don't.

157

The key with collection letters is to keep your correspondence totally business-like and professional. Be firm and clear about what you want your customers to do (for example, they should call you to discuss the matter, have payment in your hands by noon tomorrow, or contact your collection agency).

Dos and Don'ts of Writing a Business Letter

To ensure that your business letter appears both professional and direct, keep the following guidelines in mind:

Dos

➤ Do use company letterhead when corresponding on business.

➤ Do address people as Mr. and Ms. until you are sure that you are on a first-name basis. Some people are still offended if you call them by their first name without being told that it is alright to do so.

➤ Do avoid sounding stuffy in your letters by writing as if you were talking to the person directly. Say your letter aloud before sending it; if it doesn't sound natural, make changes so that it does.

➤ Do keep your letter to one or two pages on average. If it is more than that, you risk never having your letter read. People just don't have time to read a lengthy letter.

➤ Do use a serif font instead of a sans serif font. Serif fonts are easier to read.

Don'ts

➤ Don't send a cover letter out on company stationery if you're submitting a résumé. The person receiving your résumé may suspect that you regularly pilfer company property.

➤ Don't write so informally that the recipient of your letter is made to feel uncomfortable.

➤ Don't carbon copy everyone and their brother. In many cases, other people will need to have a copy of

what you mailed out (such as your human resource department, your boss, and so on), but only send it to people who absolutely need it.

➤ Don't put anything in writing that you wouldn't want to see on the front page of the *New York Times*.

➤ Don't expect someone to call you just because you asked them to in your letter. This is especially true if you are submitting a résumé; you're responsible for all follow-up.

Basic Letter Layouts

You probably have seen many letters formatted differently and wondered which one was correctly styled. Well when it comes to business letters, some leeway is given to how you decide to type your letter. However, your company may have a preference or a certain style that they prefer. To determine this, just examine a letter that has recently been sent out by someone else. Or you can simply style your letter according to one of the three most common letter formats.

The Full Block Format

This format is the easiest because everything in the letter is left justified.

Definition

Justification   How the elements are aligned on the page. Left justified means that everything is lined up on the left, with the right side of the page remaining jagged. Your other options are right justified, centered, and justified (which means that the typing on both sides of the page is straight, not jagged). You won't have to worry about where things are supposed to go on the page because you simply keep everything aligned to the left. When you are using letterhead, there is no need to type your return address.

Definition

Copy Notation   When you need to send a copy of your letter to other people, you use the symbol "cc:" at the bottom of your letter to indicate that other people are receiving it, and then you list their names in alphabetical order.

A full block format.

Your address (if needed)

Date

Address

Salutation

Body of letter

Closing

Signature
Typed name of writer
Title of writer

Typist's initials

Enclosure notation

Copy notation

Postscript

Block Format

If the full block format is a little too boring for you, you may want to use a block format. Here, some of the pieces of a letter are positioned on the right and some on the left. Only the salutation and the body of the letter are left justified—everything else is shifted to the right-hand side of the page. Notice that they are not right justified, but rather moved a few inches to the right by using the tab key.

Frequently, when you are responding to someone else's letter it helps to use a subject line. A subject line lets the reader know right away what you're writing about. It appears below the address and above the salutation, generally with the word "Subject" or "Re" followed by your topic.

A block format.

Date
Address
Subject
Salutation
Body
Close
Signature
Typed name of writer
Title
Typist's initials
Enclosure notation
Copy notation
Postscript

Semiblock

If you prefer indented paragraphs, rather than leaving everything left justified, you may want to use a semiblock format for your letters. The semiblock format looks exactly like the block layout except that the paragraphs within the letter are indented half an inch.

A semiblock format.

February 23, 1996

Ms. Marjorie Lewis
Big Blue Investments
New York, NY 10010

Dear Ms. Lewis,

I understand that my employee, Natalie Gregory, has applied for a position with your firm. Because I know that she is eager to relocate to New York and to have the opportunity to work with you, I'd like to encourage you to seriously consider her.

During the past two years that Natalie has worked with me, she has become an integral part of my business, assuming responsibility for many aspects of the operations and marketing of Market Leaders.

Partly because she is extremely bright and partly because she has an incredible amount of initiative, Natalie has become involved in virtually every aspect of running a small business.

She is the project manager for the creation and production of a new business directory, handling the information collection, analysis, production and marketing of this product. She also responds to telephone and mail inquiries for information on our business planning services, determining what information should be sent and following up on a regular basis. She researches market and industry data for clients using a variety of online and published sources. She creates financial spreadsheets for client business plans, ensuring the figures are accurate each time.

When Natalie sees something that needs to be done, she begins the work immediately, needing little, if any, supervision. She also works until the project is completed, enabling me, her employer, to feel confident that any work that needs to be done will be done.

Although I am sad to see her leave, I want to help her secure a challenging and fulfilling position with a new firm in the metro New York area. And this is the reason for my letter.

If I can answer any questions about Natalie, please feel free to contact me.

Sincerely,

Bob Smith

Blind Copy Notation

Sometimes you need to send someone a copy of a letter, but you may not want the original recipient to know it. That's called "blind copying" someone.

The symbol "bc" on the copy you're sending out secretly indicates that the person to whom the letter is addressed doesn't need to know that anyone else is getting it. Don't type "bc" on the original letter though; that defeats the purpose by letting your reader know others are seeing the letter.

When you're sending a blind copy out, type "bc" below your name at the bottom of the letter, or below any enclosure notation you may have.

Typist's Initials

In bigger companies, where secretaries often type correspondence for people, it's routine for the typist to type his or her initials below your name at the bottom of the page. This helps you track down who has the letter on their computer system if you need to find it later.

If you type your own letters, there's no need to type your own initials where a typist normally puts his or hers. You'll probably be able to remember who typed your letter and where you filed it away.

Postscript

Direct mail copywriters always use the "P.S." notation at the bottom of every letter they send because it's one of the most-read parts of a letter.

Don't make a habit of typing little postscript notes unless you're in direct marketing. But if you need to add a personal message, or want to highlight an important point in your letter, the P.S. at the bottom is the perfect place for this.

Tip
Use a P.S. to call attention to a point you want to emphasize. Studies have shown that the P.S. is the second-most read section of a letter.

Additional Pages

Often business letters fit on one single page. When they run on to additional sheets, here are a couple of formatting conventions you'll need to be aware of:

➤ First, in the top left, type "Page 2," or whatever page you happen to be on.

➤ Second, don't use letterhead except on the first page of your correspondence. Use what are called "second sheets," which are blank pieces of the paper your stationery is printed on. So the paper type matches, but it doesn't have any printing on it at all.

The Least You Need to Know

➤ Every business letter contains three major parts: the introduction, the body, and the close.

➤ Read your letter out loud before you send it to see if it sounds natural.

➤ When sending bad news, always try to start and end the letter with a statement that will make the recipient feel better.

➤ There are three basic letter formats: full block, block, and semiblock.

DEAR SIR/AND OR MADAM, HOW WOULD YOU LIKE TO MAKE A TON OF MONEY?

Chapter 19

Sales Letters

In This Chapter

➤ How to write a convincing letter

➤ Why you should focus on the customers' needs

➤ Tips on improving your chances of making a sale

➤ Sample letters

Your company may have the slickest marketing brochure in the history of mankind, but what's really going to help sell your potential customers is the letter that accompanies your brochure. That letter explains why customers should buy your product *now*. And the better it is, the faster they will buy.

You may have written thousands of letters in your career, but to write a successful sales letter takes good writing skills and lots of creativity. Here are some tips that have worked for others that you can use to improve your own sales letters.

Focus on What the Customer Cares About

The biggest secret to writing effective sales letters is to focus on what's important to your customers and potential customers. Or more specifically, what they will gain by buying from you.

Think about it—don't you get irritated at salespeople who drone on and on about stuff that you aren't even interested in? Well, that's what an ineffective sales letter does on paper. It tells potential customers what's important to you, but doesn't convince them that you understand what's important to them. And, let's be honest, they really don't care about what's important to you or your company. So unless you can convince them that you understand what they're looking for, and can explain why your product or your service meets their needs, you're out of a sale.

One way to keep the focus on your sales prospect and away from your company is to use the word "you" in place of "I" whenever possible. When you use the word "we" or "I," you are telling customers what's important to you, which they could care less about.

> ### ! Quote
>
> In any "unsolicited" communication (including articles), your success in holding the reader's interest depends heavily on the first sentence! Think of what the reader's main interest, fear, or curiosity is likely to be, and address that in a way that requires him or her to read on. One of the best ways to do that is to create a little tension by asking a question.
>
> **George R. Berman**, Berman Associates.

Tips for Writing a Better Letter

Telling your potential customers "what's in it for them" is crucial for getting them to pay attention to your sales letter, and there are other steps you can take to lead them toward a sale. Carol Nelson of Communicomp in Fort Lauderdale, Florida, makes these suggestions for improving the response to your sales letters.

➤ Make your sales prospect feel comfortable with you by pointing out things you have in common. For example, begin your greeting with "Dear Fellow Member" or "Dear Fellow Wellesley Alumna" to establish a kinship with each other.

Later in your letter, you can continue to discuss why you understand the customer's needs so well. "You and I both know that windsurfing in Aruba isn't for beginners…"

or "We've both experienced the frustrations of running a small business...." These types of phrases help your prospect feel close to you.

➤ You can never overuse the word "you" in your letter. Whenever possible, remind readers that you are talking directly to them. Instead of saying "We are making this special offer in order to clean out our warehouse to make room for new inventory," try "*You* will receive this special offer in order to clean out our warehouse to make room for new inventory."

➤ Use phrases that either sound bigger or smaller, depending on the impression you are trying to make. For instance, the unit of measure you use can influence whether customers think they're getting a good deal or not. The bigger the unit of measure, the larger the impact. For example, seven days seems like less time than one week, though we both know that time-wise they're exactly the same. The same holds true for other units of measure; sixty seconds seems less than one minute.

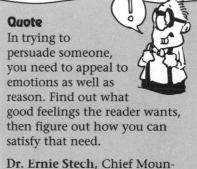

Quote

In trying to persuade someone, you need to appeal to emotions as well as reason. Find out what good feelings the reader wants, then figure out how you can satisfy that need.

Dr. Ernie Stech, Chief Mountain Consulting, Inc. in Littleton, Colorado.

So depending on which aspect you want to emphasize, use the larger or smaller unit of measure. When you offer customers a money-back guarantee, for example, you want to make them feel that they have lots of time in which to return it, so you'd phrase your offer using a larger unit of measure. Which means you'd choose to offer it for one year, rather than 12 months.

However, if you're trying to make a product appear inexpensive, use "ninety-nine cents" rather than "less than a dollar" since cents are smaller than dollars. And when there are several zeroes in a number, write it out; "one thousand" looks smaller than $1,000.00.

Of course, the reverse is true if you're talking about savings or the benefits of using your product. Then you'd want to make the number seem as large as possible.

Dos and Don'ts

Writing a successful sales letter takes time and creativity. Your sales will increase if you convince your readers to buy your product. To convince them, you have to clearly explain why they should spend their money. Some other points to keep in mind are:

Dos

➤ Do send along sales material to provide specific product or service information. Don't try to say everything there is to say about the product in a one page introductory letter. It just can't be done effectively.

➤ Do use a headline centered below the address for impact. Ask a question related to what you're selling, or make a statement expressing the benefits you can offer customers. For example, "Is your company getting the publicity it deserves?"

➤ Do use words that have been proven to increase response. These include "free," "money," "happiness," and "now."

➤ Do use a P.S. note to mention a special offer or to restate a reason to buy now. The P.S. is the second most-read section of a letter, so don't miss out.

➤ Do use a serif font instead of a sans serif. Research has shown that serif typefaces are easier to read.

Definition

Serif Typeface   One of two varieties of lettering used in typed documents. The extra lines that extend from the bottom and top of each character give this typeface a fancier look (similar computer fonts are Times and Palatino). Sans serif fonts don't have any extra curves or lines (for example, Helvetica and Futura fonts).

➤ Do end the letter with a "call to action" that tells the reader what you want them to do next. Or, if you prefer to follow up, tell them specifically when you'll do that: "in the next week," "the week of March 3rd," or "next Tuesday."

Definition

Call to Action   A phrase used in the advertising industry that refers to what you want your sales prospects to do to move the sale forward. After reading your letter do you want them to call you? Return a postcard to request more information? Visit your store on Madison Avenue? Place an order?

Don'ts

➤ Don't use negative words or phrases to try to scare customers. Positive messages work much better at getting a response and getting a sale.

➤ Don't feel that you have to fit everything into one single page. Some of the best performing sales letters are several pages in length. Of course, your printing costs do go up.

Formatting Your Letter

You now can apply what you've already learned in this book since sales letters are formatted the same way as standard business letters. If you forgot what the different layouts are for letters, just turn back to Chapter 18 for a refresher.

A sales letter is a business letter written for a specific purpose—to help close a sale. So it is formatted just as you would format any other business letter.

Date

Name and address of intended recipient

Dear _____,

Headline

First paragraph—Introduce yourself and what your company can do for your customer.

Second paragraph—Elaborate a little on all the benefits your customers will experience by working with you.

Third paragraph—Explain why you are the best.

Fourth paragraph—Thank the customer for her time and mention your call to action.

Closing,

Your name and title

P.S.

Samples

If you're thinking of rewriting one of your sales letters, or are trying to put together a new one from scratch, here are a few examples to give you some ideas:

CORPORATE SPEAKER

July 2, 1996

John Q. Public
Corporate Training Manager
Megacorp, Inc.
10 Technology Way
Anytown, DE 19807

Dear Mr. Public,

Jane Anderson thought you'd be interested in learning about my availability as a speaker for meetings of the Women's Forum of Megacorp Employees.

Specifically, as you'll see from the enclosed material, I take a humorous approach to gender dynamics in the workplace, helping men and women understand how the genders work and communicate differently. Recognizing and dealing with these differences can have a significant impact on an individual's career while enhancing the advancement of the entire organization.

For example, the typical woman does not realize that asking questions—which women view as a valid way of information gathering—is often viewed by male supervisors as an indication that the woman doesn't know enough to do her job. As a result, she doesn't receive the promotion she deserves, and the organization doesn't benefit from her talent at the next level.

My presentations—which range from a 30-minute session to a 90-minute training workshop—are unique in that they use a great deal of humor to help women understand men. I use anecdotes, cartoons, and research from my book, *Why Can't a Man Be More Like a Woman?* (Kensington, May 1995), to explain the vastly different ways typical men and women approach teamwork, problem-solving, communication, and the workplace in general.

I'd like an opportunity to meet with you to discuss your interest in a lighthearted, but information-packed program on gender dynamics which will help make employees more productive. I'll call soon to determine your interest.

Cordially,
Sandra L. Beckwith

HIGH END SECURITY SYSTEMS
April 1, 1996
John Smith
Fortune 500 Corporation
100 Corporate Drive
Anytown, MA 02110

Dear John,

Is Your Company Doing All That It Can to Safeguard Your Employees and Company Assets?

Many companies don't realize some of the simple yet effective steps that can be taken to better protect corporate employees, facilities, and corporate assets, such as equipment, artwork, or documents.

Our company, Security Products, Inc., specializes in the design and installation of integrated security systems. Even the most basic system heightens the level of security you provide to your most valuable assets—your employees.

Whether your major concern is limiting access to your facilities, identifying employees and suppliers, or controlling access to certain areas of your buildings, we can help set up such a system.

In many cases, our system can provide cost savings to your organization in addition to improved protection. Many companies find it possible to significantly reduce the cost of security personnel through the installation of our system, in addition to making remaining guards more efficient and accountable.

We can provide you with any of the following security elements as part of a complete system:

➤ Access control system
➤ Premise security monitoring
➤ Electronic art protection
➤ Video monitoring system
➤ Assistance system
➤ Video badging

We've successfully installed security systems for clients across New York State, including *Readers Digest*, Bausch & Lomb, Chase Bank, Knolls Atomic Power, and major museums.

We recognize that security is becoming a greater concern for organizations nationwide. And if it is one of your priorities, we'd like to assist you. If you'd like more information about us, just return the postage paid postcard I'm enclosing and we'll send additional materials out to you right away.

Sincerely,
Victor Hill
Enclosure

P.S. Our new video demonstrates how easy our system is to operate. Call if you'd like your own copy.

FINANCIAL SERVICES
October 18, 1995
Steve O'Connor
Widgets R Us
300 Manufacturing Blvd.
Anytown, NE 12345

Dear Steve,

Is Your Company Doing All That It Can to Recover Your Wholesale Costs of Slow Moving or Excess Inventory?

Many companies don't realize some of the simple yet effective steps that can be taken to avoid write-downs and liquidations of idle assets and excess inventory.

Our company specializes in creative and strategic methods designed to not only avoid the "loss" but enhance the market value of your distressed or obsolete inventory.

Whether your major concern is eliminating the cost of warehousing your idle product (freeing up space for higher demand and more profitable inventory) or recovering 100% of your initial investment, we can help you evaluate your options.

In many cases, our efforts can provide cost savings to your organization in addition to improving your purchasing capabilities. Many companies find it possible to make capital improvements to their facilities, upgrade their equipment, and reinvest in profitable markets by bartering their non-performing assets.

We can provide you with any of the following services as part of a complete turnkey project:

➤ On-premise assessment of current excess inventory
➤ Evaluation of the inventory's true "market value"
➤ Outsourcing of potential cash market buyers
➤ Recommendations for recovering the inventory's cost using practical barter methods
➤ Lot purchase of the inventory in exchange for accounts receivable credit
➤ Purchasing and bid proposals for budgeted capital purchases utilizing accounts receivable credit, reducing your cash outlay and preserving your operating capital

We have successfully recovered 100% of carrying costs (book or wholesale value) from a variety of industries across New York State, including but not limited to a material handling company, office supply distributor, and consumer electronics retailer.

We recognize that excess inventory is not only a burden but also a potential capital loss. If your company is interested in capturing an often overlooked revenue stream and you would rather record a gain than a loss, we'd like to assist you.

If you would like more information about us, please fax us some preliminary information about your company and we will be glad to send additional materials out to you right away.

Sincerely,

Debra Van Wert

Vice President

The Least You Need to Know

➤ Emphasizing how customers will benefit from using your product or service is the key to a successful sales letter.

➤ A headline directly below the salutation introduces your product and captures the customer's interest.

➤ Use a P.S. at the bottom of your sales letter to mention a deadline or special offer.

➤ Don't limit your letter to one page. Longer letters are often read more thoroughly.

Proposals

Every organization at some time or another has to prepare a proposal, whether it is to generate new business, apply for a government grant, or to request approval to proceed with a new project. And usually that responsibility falls on the shoulder of one capable individual. Since you're reading this chapter, you must see a proposal writing opportunity in your future.

Some people get scared by the prospect of putting a proposal together, but if you follow the guidelines in this chapter, you'll be able to prepare thorough proposals that earn serious consideration.

What Is a Proposal?

Proposals are documents prepared to try to persuade someone else to approve a project, idea, or business opportunity. They come in a number of shapes and sizes. At one end of the spectrum is the one-page informal proposal that is often requested as a follow-up to a discussion with a client. With an ongoing client relationship, there is generally no need to restate your qualifications, strength of your project team, resources, and so on because the client is already familiar with those. That's why he/she has been working with you in the first place.

And on the other end of the spectrum is the 100 page bound technical proposal that is frequently required by government agencies. In these very formal situations, every "i" must be dotted and "t" crossed or you risk being disqualified.

The one commonality across all situations is that the proposal is used as a selling document. No matter what the opportunity, you are trying to persuade someone to do something your way. The proposal is the tool you use to communicate your intentions.

> ## Quote
>
> In writing a proposal, restate the requesting party's statement of need, requirements, or work. However, use the original words and phrases as much as possible. People like to see their own phrasings come back to them. After all, that's what they understand best.
>
> **Dr. Ernie Stech**, Chief Mountain Consulting, Inc. in Littleton, Colorado.

When a Proposal Is Appropriate

In some cases, you will be asked to prepare a proposal to bid on a particular project or account and in other cases you may decide to submit a proposal on your own without having been asked.

When major corporations, government agencies, and large non-profit organizations undertake significant projects or plan large purchases, typically a Request for Proposal (RFP) is issued.

> ## Definition
>
> **Request For Proposal (RFP)**   A document prepared by an organization looking to hire a company to provide specific goods or services. The RFP outlines exactly what the company wants to purchase and why, and asks potential suppliers to respond within a certain period of time with a bid.

Responding to an RFP

The most elaborate proposal process involves submitting a proposal in response to an RFP from an organization. When you receive an RFP, you know that there is an opportunity to do some business, if you like the terms of the project that are outlined in the RFP packet. Both the information packet you receive and the proposal you're expected to put together are generally lengthy and involved. Just reading the RFP alone can take hours.

Once you've reviewed an RFP that's landed on your desk, decide first whether this is a project you even want to bid on. Just because you've received an invitation to submit a proposal does not mean that you have to. OK, maybe you personally don't want to have to put the darn proposal together, but think about whether it makes sense for your company to bid on.

If you do decide that you don't want to bid, you should at least send a short letter saying "thanks, but no thanks" so that they'll send you future RFPs. This type of letter is typically referred to as a "no bid" letter. Simply address it to the person in charge of the project and explain why your company won't be submitting a proposal. Acceptable reasons include:

> **Quote**
> Keep proposals short. If you can't get everything down in a few pages (unless it's a highly technical manufacturing or systems development project), you probably don't know the job well enough.
>
> **Terra Friedrichs**, writer.

➤ "Business is booming and we are not prepared to get involved in such a major undertaking at the current time/not able to commit the necessary resources to do the job right."

➤ "The timeline required in the RFP is not one we can work with given our current project load."

➤ "The area in which you need help is not one of our specialties."

Unacceptable reasons that you wouldn't want to state in your letter include:

➤ "Your budget is so low that no company can give you what you want."

➤ "We ran a credit check and you haven't been paying your bills so we don't want to take a chance."

➤ "We've worked with you before and vowed never to do that again."

If you do decide to submit a proposal, your proposal should be formatted according to what the organization has asked for. In some ways, an RFP makes life easier. The company or agency tells you up front exactly what they're looking for, why they think they need it, and how they're going to evaluate any proposals they receive.

Pitching a New Account

To be successful in sales, you need to constantly be uncovering new potential customers and convincing them to buy from you. Part of that process—whether you work for an advertising agency, commercial printer, or manufacturer of automotive parts—involves providing a written proposal of what your company has to offer. Prospects want to know "What can you do for me?"

Often organizations don't have the exact details worked out regarding an upcoming need for products or services, but they know they'll need something. Which is when you may have the chance to propose hiring your employer.

Unlike responding to an RFP, you won't have a lot of background regarding the company's current situation or needs. So you need to emphasize the experience and expertise of your company across a wide variety of projects and clients.

Quoting on a Project

When a current or potential client knows exactly what they're looking for, you may be asked to provide a quote to complete a certain project or provide a quantity of products.

A quote is a type of proposal that will be evaluated primarily based on price. You don't need to go into lots of details regarding your company's background and experience. You just need to state what the cost is to do a particular job, or supply however many products they need.

You also don't have to try and convince the organization that your approach is the best one—they really just want to know what it's going to cost them.

Applying for Funding

Government grants also require funding proposals. Because there is a limited amount of money to be spent on different projects and pursuits, you need to make a strong case for your particular interest.

The one major modification to take into account in these situations is that proposals made on behalf of non-profit organizations, research projects, and university studies should demonstrate the benefit to the community. The funding source often wants to understand how your use of their money is going to result in some sort of improvement in the quality of life for a group of people, or in our knowledge of a particular situation. Adding a section on the benefits of your project is a simple way to address this.

How Detailed It Needs to Be

Each proposal should look and sound like it is a unique approach to this particular organization's situation. Proposals that look like they take a cookie cutter approach—every project is tackled the same way—are rarely successful at getting desired results.

Companies, and individuals, like to feel as if they are unusual and unique. So even if you've seen dozens of situations exactly like the one you're currently faced with at this organization, treat it as if it were your first.

While each proposal will be different, there is a common outline to follow to ensure you address each major issue:

> I. Title page
>
> II. Table of contents
>
> III. Executive summary
>
> IV. Description of current situation
>
> V. Recommended solution
>
> VI. Explanation of your approach (how you'll get the work done)
>
> VII. Cost and timeline
>
> VIII. Why your company is best qualified
>
> IX. Appendices

Quote
When writing a proposal, list the major requirements as "bullets." Then proceed to show how you can meet each of those requirements. I have even provided customers with a checklist so that they could check off the requirements as I showed how we would accomplish them.

Dr. Ernie Stech, Chief Mountain Consulting, Inc. in Littleton, Colorado.

Title Page

Your title page is simply the cover sheet to your proposal that helps identify what the proposal is for and who submitted it. So the crucial pieces of information on any title page are the description of your proposal and your company's name. You may also want to add the name of the company that is receiving the proposal—partly to make them feel good about seeing their name on the cover and partly to help you keep track of which proposal is which. The date on which you're submitting the proposal is also helpful to note on the title page.

Table of Contents

To help readers find information quickly and easily, it always makes sense to include a table of contents in all your proposals. It also makes you appear very organized, which is a plus.

Tip

Many computer word processing programs have a built-in Table of Contents feature that allows you to mark which headings should be part of the table of contents. Once they're all marked, you just type a command and the table is created automatically, complete with updated page references.

Executive Summary

The first section of a proposal should be a one- to two-page summary of the entire proposal. Write this section last, once you've put everything else down on paper in a logical fashion.

Definition
Synopsis A synopsis is not an introduction; it is an overview of the whole proposal.

The point of an executive summary is to provide a brief synopsis of the proposal, so that if a busy executive only had time to read two pages, they could read the summary and generally understand what you're proposing.

Current Situation

Start your proposal by showing your potential customers that you understand their particular situation. Restate what they've told you about the problems and challenges they face.

Many RFPs will have a background section giving you some details regarding why the organization is considering hiring a supplier to help them out.

If you have additional information that you can use to support their own description, use it. For example, if you have industry data, statistics, or a recent article related in some way to the challenge they're facing, quote it in this section.

By bringing in information from outside sources, you also appear to have thoroughly researched their situation in order to come up with your proposed solution, which you describe in the next section.

Recommended Solution

After reviewing what the problem is, you can then propose a solution. However, make sure that the solution you are suggesting is one that your company can provide. This is a seemingly obvious point that companies sometimes forget.

You don't have to explain yet how you are going to achieve results for the company; just tell them what they need to do.

For example, if you've been asked to provide a solution to the challenge of introducing a new product with a budget of $10,000, you would describe in this section how that can be achieved. Part of that solution might include giving up on paid advertisements at the outset and relying more heavily on product sampling, publicity, and consumer shows in order to generate interest in the product.

Your Approach

Once you've explained what you believe the company should do to address its needs and situation, you need to provide some detail regarding how you're going to help the company do that. This is the section where you outline the process or methodology you'll use to get the job done.

You don't have to give the company all the answers so that they're able to go off and complete the work without you, but you do need to reassure them that you know what you're doing. Telling a prospective company that your process will complete a project for them is different from telling them what each individual step involves.

To continue with the product introduction challenge described above, in this section you would explain how you would go about providing product samples (such as by hand delivering them to major prospects), getting national publicity (such as by creating a press kit and several press releases), and attending consumer shows (which might include a press conference at the biggest annual show).

If you just provide a recommended solution without telling the organization how you propose to complete the project, you may leave some doubt as to whether you can really pull it off.

You have an advantage when you know which other companies may also be bidding on the job. You can then weave references to their weaknesses into your proposal without mentioning them by name. For example, if your product offers a feature that your competitors don't, you can emphasize the importance of this particular feature throughout your proposal. Or if they service customers through subcontractors, rather than full-time employees, you can bring up how big a difference that can make. Emphasize the positives of what your company has to offer and that your competition cannot.

Quote
Make every subhead an action sentence with a positive verb in it. For example, instead of saying "XYZ Capabilities Statement," say "XYZ has the capabilities this project demands" or "XYZ Capabilities will make this project shine."

Linda Stern, professional writer and syndicated personal finance columnist.

181

Cost and Timeline

Many RFPs require that you put any cost or budget information in a totally separate document, so that it can be evaluated apart from the content of your proposal. If this is the case, you'll just want to pull this section out and make it a stand-alone document.

If you're offering a proposal or providing a quote that someone has asked for, you'll want to keep it together with the other information.

Your cost information may consist of separate line items for major parts of the project or a lump sum for the whole enchilada. Professionals, such as consultants, attorneys, and accountants, frequently quote in terms of hours, along with an hourly rate, rather than a project fee.

In situations where a company is facing a looming deadline, whether you can meet their schedule for delivery may be of more importance than your pricing. Break down the major sections of the project and estimate how long each section will take to complete. You can do this in writing, or visually with the help of a chart. See Chapter 14 for more information on using charts to make your point visually.

Company Experience

To reinforce the impression that your company is highly qualified to complete the proposed project, provide information in this section on the personnel assigned to work on the project. Briefly describe their backgrounds, education, and experiences to-date that make them desirable members of the project team.

Also highlight other clients and projects your company has worked on, especially where the project was similar to the one being proposed. If your company specializes in a particular niche, vertical market, or has expertise in a certain area, also describe that here.

Appendices

To keep your proposal as easy to read as possible, it often makes sense to group all of your exhibits and supporting material in a separate section in the back of the proposal. Typical information found in the Appendix includes:

➤ Staff résumés

➤ Corporate marketing materials

➤ Corporate client list

➤ Work samples

➤ Illustrations

➤ Blueprints

What It Should Look Like

Following are a few sample pages found in a typical proposal:

ABC Widgets

Proposal to Develop a Marketing Campaign for the New Widget2000

January 1997

Prepared by:
Jones & Jones

The title page.

TABLE OF CONTENTS

The table of contents page.

Recommended Tactics

MARKETING STRATEGIES

In this section, you would detail the marketing methods you intend to use as they relate to this proposal.

ADVERTISING

Under this heading you would cover the specific actions you believe the reader should take relative to advertising. How specific you get in your recommendations varies by situation and by client.

SPECIAL PROMOTIONS

Here, of course, you'd detail your recommendations relative to special promotions you believe this prospect should seriously consider.

PUBLIC RELATIONS

I usually go a little overboard when discussing PR, so if I were writing this, it would probably be the longest section in the whole proposal.

TELEMARKETING

Any use of telemarketers in your project should be described in this section.

TRADE SHOWS

The trade shows that you think your potential client should attend would be listed here, along with any exhibit-related activities.

This is the last page in my demonstration, but I wanted to at least give you an idea of what a completed proposal might look like. You can experiment with designing your pages; the key is choosing a standard layout for all the pages and being consistent throughout.

An example of the inside pages of your proposal.

Dos and Don'ts

While there are a variety of proposal formats, there are standard dos and don'ts common to all proposals.

Dos

➤ Do make sure that your proposal addresses all the requirements set forth in the request for proposal you're responding to.

Tip
Binding a proposal improves its professional appearance. There are several types of inexpensive binding options available at most copy shops: plastic spiral binding, adhesive tape binding, and hard cover ChannelBinding.

➤ Do decide up-front if this proposal is even worth putting together. Some opportunities aren't worth pursuing because of the time and effort required just to bid.

➤ Do pay attention to the impression your proposal gives. The look and feel of a document does impact how your company is viewed.

➤ Do proofread and double check your proposal for errors before sending it out. One blatant mistake and you seriously jeopardize any potential contract.

➤ Do send along a cover letter to your contact person thanking him/her for the opportunity to submit a proposal.

➤ Do make sure your proposal is straightforward and easy-to-read.

➤ Do use specifics when referring to your experience. For instance, "Our client base of 400 of the Fortune 500" is more credible than "We have many installations worldwide."

➤ Do use color and graphics to emphasize important points.

Don'ts

➤ Don't start writing until you have mapped out an outline for how you're going to meet the client's needs.

➤ Don't go overboard with technical jargon and verbiage; stick to plain English for ease of understanding.

➤ Don't overdo it with fonts and typestyles; two is plenty, three is the absolute maximum.

➤ Don't mention your competitors by name in your proposal, even if you know who you're bidding against.

Samples

BRUGNONI DESIGN

To: Incredible Products, Inc.
99 Fast Lane
P. O. Box 909
Pittsford, NY 14534
Att. John Goodguy

Date: April 25, 1996

P.O. Number:

Due Date: May 15, 1996

Description:	Amount
Thomas Register Negatives & Photography	
Four Stock Photo Shots	$1,840.00
Press Proof/Blue Line Check	$ 200.00
Film Negatives for Thomas Registry	$ 240.00
Positioning photography in layout for printer	$ 295.00
Photography - Four shots plus two extra	$1,490.00
Coordination Fee	$ 250.00
Photo Art Direction	$ 400.00
Subtotal	$4,715.00
Sales Tax (If tax exempt, please send tax ID Number.)	$ 377.20

TERMS: SERVICE CHARGE OF 2% PER MONTH ADDED AFTER 30 DAYS. IN THE EVENT OF NON-PAYMENT, **ALL** COLLECTION COSTS (INCLUDING ANY LEGAL EXPENSES AND COURT FEES) WILL BE THE RESPONSIBILITY OF THE BUYER.

Total $5,092.20

19 Laureldale Drive Pittsford, NY 14534 (716) 264.9964 Fax: (716) 264.0147

An example of a quote.

SOL 104230-92-A-0012

TECHNICAL PROPOSAL

Newspaper Columns and Radio Releases
SOL 104230-92-A-0012
Due: 12/9/97 4:00 pm

U.S. Postal Service
Office of Procurement, Room 4541
475 L'Enfant Plaza, SW
Washington, DC 20260-6237

Smith Jones Advertising Agency
123 Main Street
Omaha, NE 12345

A government publicity proposal.

SOL 104230-92-A-0012

TABLE OF CONTENTS

2

SOL 104230-92-A-0012

PROJECT APPROACH

Smith Jones believes that there are two essential components to the success of the U.S. Postal Service's contract for the preparation of newspaper columns and radio releases.

One component is the quality of the writing. Our years of experience in working with the media to obtain coverage for our clients has taught us that top quality writing is essential to having information utilized in both the print and broadcast media. Articles and releases must be well-written, appropriate, and interesting in order to obtain placement in the news media.

For this reason we have established an agreement with Jane O'Brien of Writing Specialists to provide all writing and editing of the U.S. Postal Service columns and releases. Jane O'Brien is experienced in writing and editing articles and releases. In addition, as a quality control mechanism, O'Brien will route all written materials through our offices for review and approval before being forwarded to the Postal Service. We believe this two-step approach to creation of the materials will ensure higher quality writing, fewer revisions needed by the Postal Service, and increased number of placements.

The second component vital to the successful placement of the U.S. Postal Service's columns and releases is the nationwide media distribution channel. Access to newspapers and radio stations across the country is critical.

To provide this access we will utilize the services of Media USA, which has a production and distribution system in place to efficiently distribute and track all news columns and radio releases issued on behalf of the Postal Service. Media USA will work with Smith Jones to provide accurate statistical reports and updates to the Postal Service as clips arrive.

Smith Jones believes that excellent writing skills and a fresh approach to the column format combined with a nationwide media distribution service will provide the U.S. Postal Service with superior results in terms of placements and consumer feedback.

Our approach to this contract emphasizes preparing creative columns and releases that will generate placements. While nationwide media distribution systems are an excellent means of disseminating publicity materials, they often take a "cookie-cutter" approach to writing releases. We can produce higher quality, more dynamic columns and releases that will get picked up by editors. We believe the superiority of our writing abilities will result in numbers of clippings beyond the minimum quantity of 100.

3

SOL 104230-92-A-0012

DISCUSSION

Upon notification of contract award and receipt of information for use in determining topics for the news columns and radio releases, Smith Jones will review the information for completeness and forward it to Jane O'Brien.

Based on input from the U.S. Postal Service and Smith Jones, O'Brien will then write draft copy for the news columns and/or releases. She will route the draft to Smith Jones for review and approval. Smith Jones will then forward the draft to the U.S. Postal Service within one week of receipt of the topical information. The U.S. Postal Service will review the draft, edit and revise as they deem appropriate, and return it to Smith Jones within 2 weeks.

Smith Jones and O'Brien will discuss the requested changes and either implement them immediately and return the final copy to the USPS within 5 days for final approval *or* contact the USPS representative immediately with any questions or concerns regarding the revisions. This additional contact will only occur if Smith Jones believes that the proposed revisions may jeopardize the amount of placements the column or release will receive. Because the level of placements is essential to the success of the contract, we request permission to discuss changes that we do not believe are in the best interests of the USPS, based on our experience in working with the media.

On receipt of final approval from the USPS, Smith Jones will forward the column/release to Media USA for typesetting. Smith Jones will forward the final typeset columns to the Postal Service, who will return the approved columns within 5 days.

Media USA will be responsible for nationwide distribution of the newspaper features on U.S. Postal Service topics to 8,000 daily and weekly newspaper editors and news and wire services. Media USA will also provide collection of clippings and initial preparation of readership reports for analysis by Smith Jones. Smith Jones will check the information for accuracy and completeness and prepare a final report with usage figures, newspaper names, locations, and readership demographics for the USPS.

The first status report will occur *either* when the minimum number of news clippings (100) or radio response cards (200) is received by Smith Jones, in which case it would be the final and only report on that particular column or release, *or* an initial status report will be issued after three months has elapsed, at which time Smith Jones will provide an update on how many clippings or response cards have been received to date and usage figures for those media. These status reports will continue on a monthly basis until the minimum number of clippings or response cards is received and a final report is issued by Smith Jones. Copies of all response cards will be included with the status reports for USPS verification purposes.

4

SOL 104230-92-A-0012

SUBCONTRACTING RELATIONSHIPS

Smith Jones will utilize the skills of freelance writer Jane O'Brien, principal of Writing Specialists, to write the news columns and radio releases in support of the U.S. Postal Service's needs.

WRITING SPECIALISTS

Writing Specialists is a small, woman-owned business established in 1989 to provide marketing consulting services, including writing and editing of business communications.

Principal Jane O'Brien has experience within communications organizations of both entrepreneurial and Fortune 500 corporations, where she had responsibility for writing and managing public relations and marketing communications programs. These writing assignments have included press releases, articles, newsletters, and press kits. Her volunteer work with the American Diabetes Association has involved writing radio releases for local radio stations.

In addition, she is currently under contract to complete a non-fiction book to be published in early 1998 by The Consultant Press, Ltd. Her proposal for this project was selected by the publisher based on the high quality of her writing and expertise in marketing.

Samples of her writing are attached in Appendix A.

MEDIA USA

A promotional package describing Media USA's expertise in production and distribution follows this section.

Media USA places news features in newspapers nationwide. They distribute news to a nationwide database of editors at dailies, weeklies, and other newspapers. In addition, Radio USA distributes news releases to radio stations nationwide. Clipping and readership/usage reports are also provided as part of Media USA services.

5

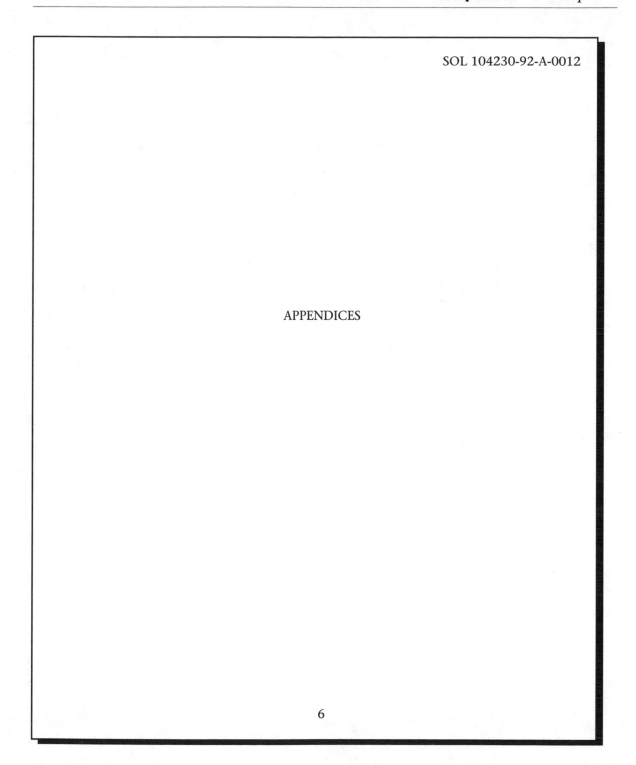

SOL 104230-92-A-0012

APPENDICES

6

SOL 104230-92-A-0012

Appendix A

Writing Samples

Appearing on the next pages are samples of work written by Smith Jones and Jane O'Brien of Writing Specialists. Included in the package are press releases, radio releases, and articles.

7

SOL 104230-92-A-0012

Appendix B

Relevant Experience

PROJECT MANAGEMENT

Smith Jones' project management experience is varied and successful, and includes managing an award-winning national program with a budget of nearly $400,000 spent on special events and publicity across the country, and publicizing a sports award program by sending more than 50 customized press releases to the hometown and college media of the award nominees.

WRITING/EDITING

Jane O'Brien, a freelance writer, has had experience in a wide range of writing assignments, from writing and editing a non-fiction book, to researching and preparing corporate press releases, radio releases, newsletters, expertise articles, and case histories which have been published in daily newspapers and trade media, to copywriting for marketing brochures and literature. Additionally, she has prepared audio-visual presentations, coordinated multifaceted public relations campaigns, and managed large communications programs.

8

SOL 104230-92-A-0012

Appendix C

Samples of Placement Results

Enclosed is a copy of the publicity generated for a project Smith Jones created, managed, and publicized for four years.

9

SOL 104230-92-A-0012

Appendix D

Qualifications of Key Personnel

SMITH JONES ADVERTISING AGENCY

Susan Jones, principal of Smith Jones, has 16 years of public relations and journalism experience, including assignments as a contributing editor of three trade journals. In addition to writing and placing countless press releases in her career, Jones has continually contributed freelance articles to a wide range of consumer and trade magazines, including three with *Home Office Computing* in the past 12 months. Her work has also appeared in *Mademoiselle, Cosmopolitan, Ford Times, Let's Live,* and many other magazines and daily newspapers.

Her project management experience is varied and successful, and includes managing an award-winning national program with a budget of nearly $400,000 spent on special events and publicity across the country, and publicizing a sports award program by sending more than 50 customized press releases to the hometown and college media of the award nominees.

Jones has a degree in public relations and journalism from Utica College, a division of Syracuse University.

WRITING SPECIALISTS

Jane O'Brien, freelance writer and principal of Writing Specialists, has held a variety of positions in the communications departments at a variety of firms, ranging from entrepreneurial ventures to a Fortune 500 corporation. Her responsibilities have included developing integrated marketing communications programs and have involved writing ad copy, brochure text, public relations articles and releases, newsletters, and marketing presentations. As a result of these responsibilities she has had work published in several trade journals, including *Advanced Imaging, 9-1-1 Magazine, Access Control,* and *Crime Prevention Technology*, as well as numerous daily newspapers.

O'Brien earned her B.A. from Babson College and an M.B.A. from Harvard University.

10

SOL 104230-92-A-0012

Appendix E

Review of Statistical Reports

Usage and clipping reports are routinely provided to Smith Jones clients, according to the clients' specifications and information needs. Typically these reports contain information on publication name, circulation figures, column inches, and equivalent ad value calculations, but are customized to meet client needs by adding or removing report items whenever necessary.

Attached are sample reports to illustrate the type and quality of information that would be provided to the U.S. Postal Service following receipt of news clippings. In addition, copies of standard radio response cards are also included. Reports on radio usage would include the city, state, and market name, the station's call letters, the name of the individual completing the response card to report usage, a coverage map, and calculation of broadcast results at ad rates.

11

SOL 104230-92-A-0012

Appendix F

Smith Jones References

PAST/PRESENT CLIENTS

Cliff Lewis
Associate Marketing Manager
ABC Company
Thornell Road
Hartford, CT 06000
(203) 123-4567

Bob Flanagan
Major Products Corp.
456 Main Street
Buffalo, NY 14321
(716) 555-5555

12

199

The Least You Need to Know

➤ The purpose of a proposal is to sell your company's products or services to solve a prospective client's problem.

➤ Proposals can range from informal one-page letters to bound documents inches thick.

➤ The key to a strong proposal is making sure you understand the organization's problems and needs before you begin to write.

➤ A quote is a type of proposal that is evaluated primarily based on price. Stating the price alone and the specifications of the job is enough.

➤ There is a standard format you can follow that will apply to virtually every type of proposal situation.

IT'S A, UM, A GREAT SPIRAL BINDER.

Chapter 21

Reports

In This Chapter

➤ How to report results

➤ The importance of objectivity and fairness

➤ How to make effective recommendations

Remember back in high school when you had to write book reports to convince your English teacher that you had actually read the book? Well, reports are papers you have to write at the end of any project that informs people what you learned. Sometimes the project is as simple as looking into why your company paid for a shipment of products that was never delivered. And in other cases, especially with scientific and technical research, you may be preparing a document that will expand our current understanding of how things work. Whenever you want to communicate what you did and what you learned, a report is the best format to use.

Unlike proposals, in which you are trying to persuade someone to do something, reports are more of an objective account of what happened. Yes, you can still use reports to sway people's opinion one way or another, but the real purpose is to tell your story fairly and truthfully. And good report writers analyze a particular problem and come up with ideas regarding what you should do now that you have this new information.

How to Report Results

There are two types of reports. One provides the results of a research project or investigation while the other type gives new information on a topic of interest to a particular audience. However, all reports are formatted the same.

Tip
Many subscription newsletters today are a form of a report because they give subscribers the newest information on subjects such as tax reform, marketing tactics, or executive compensation. In fact, many newsletters include the word "report" in the title, indicating their intention to give readers the newest information on a topic.

A complete report includes the following sections:

➤ Cover page

➤ Table of Contents

➤ Executive Summary

➤ Research Methodology

➤ Findings

➤ Recommendations

➤ Appendix

➤ Endnotes or Works Cited

➤ Bibliography or Works Referenced

Occasionally you may find that you should leave out a section or two, or perhaps that you need to add one more because you have information that doesn't fit elsewhere. But if you follow this outline, you can be confident that you've addressed all the major issues.

Cover Page

Your report's cover page should list the title of your report, which should give an indication of what you were studying. For example, if you've been asked to investigate whether your company should increase its advertising spending this year, you might title your report "Report on Advertising Spending at XYZ Company."

On your cover page you should also list your name, the names of any team members assisting you with the research or the report-writing, your department's name, and the date on which you presented the report.

Table of Contents

The table of contents is always formatted the same way—the names of section headings on the left and the corresponding page numbers on the right.

You can get a little creative with the placement of the "Table of Contents" heading by left justifying it or centering it, underlining it, or making the type bold. Or you can add dots between each heading and its page number. Many word processing programs produce tables of contents in this fashion, with a dotted line between the section and page number.

Executive Summary

An executive summary is a short (1–2 page) synopsis of the entire project. Briefly describe what you did, how you did it, why you did it, and what you learned. The executive summary is the first section of your report because many people may not have the time to read your whole report, so they'll rely on the executive summary to get the gist of what you discovered.

One strategy for making sure you hit all the key pieces of information is to write one to two paragraphs for each section in your report. Keeping your executive summary under two pages helps ensure that it is a short summary, rather than a lengthy introduction, which you don't want.

Research Methodology

Although finding out what you discovered is often the most interesting part of any report, learning how you reached those findings is just as important. In scientific and medical research, the methodology section is considered almost as important as the findings, believe it or not. While that's not necessarily the case with business reports, the section is definitely going to be read.

Let's say that you've been asked to investigate a foolproof way to make money in the stock market. So you do your research and you report that investors can't lose if they buy stocks only on Tuesdays. People reading your report may be fascinated at this revelation, and they'll probably wonder how you came to that conclusion. So they'll flip back to your methodology section to find out. Suddenly, how you arrived at this momentous finding is as important as your investment strategy. And if your readers learn that your research involved studying the number of

> **Tip**
> Organizing your report is easier when you use 3×5 cards to take notes. Write a single thought or observation on each card, rather than several on one. When you start to prepare your report you just have to organize your cards and begin writing.

> **Quote**
> Write out what you are going to communicate in an executive summary at the beginning. Prepare the reader. Write the "meat" of the message. Then write a shorter summary at the end.
>
> **Dr. Ernie Stech**, Chief Mountain Consulting, Inc. in Littleton, Colorado.

letters in the names of profitable stock offerings, your report will be viewed with more than a little skepticism.

Since people need to understand how you logically investigated each aspect of your report, you'll need to tell them:

Definition
Random Sample A research practice that involves selecting research participants at random, rather than choosing specific people for one reason or another. Your research results are considered more accurate and reliable (believable) with random sampling.

➤ During what period of time you were conducting your research. (From August 1-31? All of last year? How long did you study whatever it was that you were studying?)

➤ How many different items you studied. (Did you study the accounting practices of five corporations or 50? Did you review 70 files or 700? How big a project was this?)

➤ How you chose what you studied. (Did you randomly sample 25 names from a company directory? Did you choose only people who retired during the month of July? What were the criteria?)

➤ Exactly what you were looking for. (Were you in search of discrepancies in payment dates? Missing check numbers? What was the subject of your research?)

Tip
Make your headings stand out by typing them in all caps or in bold.

In your methodology section, don't get into what you learned yet, just what you did as part of your investigation. The next section is when you start to reveal your findings.

Findings

Finally, after describing how you looked into the topic at hand, you can get to the meat of your report—what you discovered.

Break up each major section into separate categories using headings. For example, if some of your findings relate to finances, some to marketing, and some to research and development, create three headings to lead off each section.

Then describe what you learned about each section. Did you uncover some duplication of effort across two departments in your company? Did you find that your budget had been charged with expenses from another department by mistake? Were you able to select a new corporate attorney based on proposals submitted by three firms?

When writing up your findings, always keep in mind what the purpose of the report is. Why are you working on this project to begin with?

If you come across some new information that seems questionable, you may want to do some outside research to support your findings. This involves going to the library or logging on to an online service to locate relevant material.

For example, if your findings suggest that employees within your company feel that they are being kept in the dark about important decisions, you may want to locate other companies who have dealt with a similar situation. Information on their experiences may prove useful in deciding how your company should handle its own.

Tip
Use a footnote or endnote when you need to credit another researcher or author for an idea or statement.

Recommendations

Now comes the most important section of your report—discussing what all these findings mean for your company. After all, it doesn't really matter what you discovered. What does matter is how it affects your employer.

If you found that companies in your industry are signficantly cutting their research and development budgets, that is interesting information. But how you believe your company should respond, given this new information, is even more important.

For instance, should your company also cut its budget and save some money like everyone else? Should it go on the offensive and invest heavily for the next five years to get ahead of everyone else that is cutting back? Or should the company continue to spend what it had planned and cut back in other areas to remain competitive?

In this section, you need to decide what makes the most sense for your company, which means you are really going beyond just reporting what you did, or what you learned. You're taking a step forward and doing an analysis.

When developing your recommendations think about the following questions:

➤ What problems does this information help solve?

➤ Does it explain why some problems or situations already exist?

➤ Does it suggest new ideas that your company hasn't tried before? How can your company incorporate them into how it works?

➤ How can this information help your company earn more money or operate more effectively?

➤ Based on this new information, how can your company do things differently?

Appendix

Supporting documents that don't need to be made a part of your report should be placed in the appendix. Don't go overboard with the number of documents you use, but any technical notes, diagrams, large charts, résumés, marketing materials, budgets, and financial information should go here.

Think of the appendix as a catch-all for information that is related to your report, but which isn't crucial. If it was crucial, you would have quoted it in the body of your report.

Endnotes

Some people prefer to use footnotes within their report to reference quotes from other authors or researchers. However, if you decide that footnotes break up the flow of a report, you can lump them all together at the end of the report in the form of endnotes.

Definition
Endnotes Footnote references that are listed together at the end of a report, rather than within the document.

Just as with footnotes, the proper way to reference articles and quotes made by others is as follows:

Author's last name, author's first name, title of book, name of publisher (from book's title page) city where book was published, copyright date, pages where information originally appeared.

Tip

If you find that you are repeatedly referencing the same book or article, you can save time by typing "Ibid" in place of a footnote reference. You must type the complete reference at least once on each page, but then every reference after that can read "Ibid." If you are referencing the same book, but a different page from the previous footnote, just type "Ibid, p. ____," with the appropriate page number added.

Bibliography

If you referred to other books or articles in your report, you need to give them credit. Do this by listing the author and book in the bibliography at the end of the report. The correct way to cite each book is:

Author's last name, author's first name, title of book, name of publisher, city where book was published, copyright date.

If you reference magazine articles, the correct way to list them is:

Author's last name, author's first name, "name of article," *name of magazine or journal*, volume number, issue date.

Dos and Don'ts

Follow these tips to keep yourself out of report-writing trouble:

Dos

➤ Do write in a more formal tone, rather than the conversational style you might use in an internal memo.

➤ Do keep in mind who will be reading this report—internal staff members, technical personnel, or people outside the company, such as the board of directors, your advertising agency, or customers. Then write so that your audience is sure to understand everything you're saying.

Don'ts

➤ Don't use words like "feel" or "think," which suggest that the report is not based on fact.

➤ Don't refer to yourself or the project team in the report by using "I" or "we." This makes your statements sound like they are someone's personal opinion.

What It Should Look Like

The look and feel of a report should be one of credibility and believability. You don't have to spend big bucks on impressive bindings and graphics, but do be sure that it looks professional.

Type your report on white, bond paper. Check to be sure your printer or typewriter ribbon is in good shape, so that the letters are clear and dark. If you have the option, use a laser printer rather than a dot matrix model; the printing is clearer and looks more professional.

Single spacing can make your information seem squished together, so unless you've been instructed otherwise, try one-and-a-half spacing or even double spacing. It creates more white space between the lines which makes your report appear cleaner and not so crammed.

Use headings to separate sections and to alert the reader to what they are going to learn about. When naming sections, be consistent in your format. For example, either use single words, phrases, or complete sentences in all sections—don't mix them up for variety, because it just gets confusing.

The following are a few sample report pages:

The Effect of Oxygen on Infant Lungs

March 1998

by
Christopher Smith, M.D.
City Hospital

The cover page.

Table of Contents

The table of contents page.

EXECUTIVE SUMMARY

This is just one type of format that sets the body of your executive summary off by one inch. By indenting everything in this manner, you allow headings to stand out.

First Heading

By moving your heading flush left, it appears more prominent. It also helps break up the text in the report.

Other tricks to try include using subheadings—headings within headings.

Subheading

By moving it in only one-half inch, instead of all the way out to the left, like the heading, you create a category within a category. A subheading is similar to a "B" heading, or a second-level heading in an outline.

Don't get much fancier than this or you shift emphasis from your words to the look of your page. But when done well, the format of your report enhances the appearance and the readability of what you've written.

The executive summary page.

Presenting Your Findings

In some cases, the written report is just one part of your task making a formal presentation of your findings may be another.

Creating an oral presentation after you've written your report should be fairly simple. You should follow the same format when putting together your presentation. The difference is that you need to consider how it will look visually to your audience. Presenting your findings on an overhead cell or transparency requires that you identify the major points and reduce them down to phrases, rather than full sentences. Use these phrases to guide you through your presentation, as cues. Bullet points are frequently used to break up text, as are charts and illustrations.

Samples

Online Printing
Market Research Report

April 1995

Printing Consultants, Inc.

A market research report.

TABLE OF CONTENTS

METHODOLOGY

When conducting market research, two different methods can be used: primary research and secondary research. Primary research involves designing a unique survey instrument that is used to gather information directly from businesses and individuals. The information gathered is not already available anywhere in published form and generally is costly to collect. Secondary research, which is the technique used in this project, involves using already-published information to learn about a particular topic or opportunity. Secondary research is no less useful than primary research, but it is less costly and less time-consuming.

To gather more reported data on new trends in the printing industry that may impact USA Printers, Printing Consultants searched for articles, reports, and published findings on the following topics: printing, online industry, home-based businesses, and new printer products. Databases used to conduct these information searches include ProQuest, ABI/Inform, and Lexis/Nexis.

All articles and reports identified that contained information on those topics were printed, reviewed, analyzed, and will be summarized here for further use in the market analysis section of the company's business plan.

The findings of this research are summarized on the following pages.

3

SUMMARY

Printing Industry

The printing industry continues to experience moderate growth, with technological advances shaping the cost, quality, and delivery of printing services.

Industry Size and Growth

Commercial printing revenues grew close to 3% in the last year to over $47 billion (SOURCE: 1994 U.S. Industry Outlook).

According to *Folio Magazine*, the technological revolution that is reshaping American business has arrived at your local printer, promising to streamline the process all the way from customer service through distribution. Some of the latest developments in hardware and software that are improving quality, cutting costs, and helping publishers deliver a more targeted product are:

➤ Production software to enable communication between printers (PROSE-production order specification/EDD). Using the PROSE protocol, a record of exactly what is to be printed and how it is to be printed is submitted to the printer.

➤ Another development is that printers can now track a job from one end of the production cycle to the other, providing up-to-date status reports. Customers can access information on the status of their order 24 hours a day by modem.

➤ Estimating is also easier through an online order entry system where various components are entered and a price is calculated.

➤ Improvements in digital proofing will soon make offset filmless printing a reality (SOURCE: *Folio*, October 1993).

4

According to Modern Office Technology, digital duplicators are making inroads into the office market because they are cost-effective for over 20 copies, use less energy, are easier to maintain, and don't cost as much. For smaller volume users, a copier is the answer.

Printer Technology

ABC Company's duplicator, the Printer 6000, takes jobs that are burning out copiers and short-run jobs considered small for an offset press, and bring them in-house so users can handle the printing themselves. Duplicators are often used for newsletters, fliers, and notices that may have to go company-wide but don't need to go offset. For print runs of 1,000 or more, costs go down to $1/_3$ of a cent per copy with a Printer 6000 duplicator.

Printer 6000 technology combines digital facsimile scanning; copier electronics; and a self-contained, fully automated, high-speed printing system. This technology does not actually replace either copiers or offset printing, but it does work in conjunction with both and can save time and money.

Duplicator technology is much like that of a mimeograph where a paper master is made and used as the base. Because the cost to produce a master is so low (about 20 cents each), there is no need to keep large quantities of printed forms on hand. The Printer 6000 can produce forms on demand quickly and easily. These include short run flat forms, NCR sets, index cards, and envelopes.

In addition to the Printer 6000 duplicator, the Publisher unit links a Printer 6000 to an IBM or Macintosh system, combining desktop publishing with duplicating technology and allowing forms to be scanned into the computer and printed on the printer. The Publisher integrates high-speed printing, input scanning of text and documents, and stand-alone duplicating.

Because it uses digital technology, the Printer 6000 is also able to double as a cheap large-run printer for computers. ABC has a 55% share of the market for lithographic copiers (SOURCE: *Euromoney*, February 1994).

5

Online Industry

Today there is a rapid expansion of online computer networks. Online networks are going to reshape the way information is delivered and distributed. This expansion of online communication is impacting the way that companies do business with each other, enabling geographically disperse businesses to partner or service companies in other parts of the country, or world. In the printing industry, this drastically expands a printer's service area.

Many executives in the graphic arts community are not concerned, at the least for the moment, about the delivery and retrieval of information by means of digital technologies. But commercial printers, regardless of the markets they serve, should be concerned: electronic delivery of documents is a growing trend and one that should be tracked by printers. Recent seminars by Seybold Boston and On Demand Digital Printing & Publishing saw increased momentum for the electronic delivery of information (SOURCE: *Graphic Arts Monthly*, July 1994).

Being connected online is more than a telecommunications link using a modem, though that is a necessary requirement. Being connected has more to do with making use of online resources. In fact, supplying physical connections to the Internet has become a multimillion dollar industry in itself, valued at over $70 million in 1994 and will double by the end of 1995 (SOURCE: *Forbes*, October 1994).

Over 20 million households are on the Internet (SOURCE: *Business Week*, November 1994).

Only 10% of computer households and about 5% of U.S. households are now online, indicating significant growth potential.

Online services continue to aggressively pursue new subscribers. CompuServe has over 2 million subscribers, America Online has 1.5 million, Prodigy has 1.2 million, and Delphi and other services provide Internet access to hundreds of thousands of households. It is anticipated that in the next couple of years there will be fewer than five services left (SOURCE: *Advertising Age*, October 1994).

6

Competition

Printers are only now beginning to adopt online tools for use in their business. Two in particular are using online capabilities as a competitive advantage.

Alphagraphics, Inc. is a quickprinting franchisor. R.R. Donnelley & Sons acquired a 25% interest in Alphagraphics and has an option to acquire a majority interest.

In September 1994, Graphics Express, a Boston electronic prepress production printer, initiated a new print-on-demand service for its clients using an Agfa Chromapress digital printing press. A separate entity has been established to handle the needs of customers wanting on-demand printing (SOURCE: *Graphic Arts Monthly*, August 1994).

Home Office Market

Due to corporate cutbacks and an increasing interest in autonomy, the number of home-based businesses is increasing steadily each year. And in a related vein, service businesses, such as consulting firms, advertising agencies, and financial houses, are relying more on independent contractors and freelancers. These "virtual corporations" often use online services to communicate and to do business.

43.2 million Americans (about $1/_3$ of the workforce) are working at least part of the time from a home office in 1994. 12.7 million of them are primarily self-employed. Link Resources predicts that the home worker will increase by roughly 15% a year, to reach 56 million in 1997 (SOURCE: *The New York Times*, September 1994).

According to a survey conducted by Yankelovich Partners in 1993, 15 million full-time, home-based businesses exist in the U.S. Part-time self-employed people account for another seven million households (SOURCE: *Telephony*, February 1993).

7

218

RESULTS

What these findings mean for USA Printers is that recent industry trends are converging in support of cost-effective, online business services, such as printing. Increasing usage of online services and computer technology by businesses, and especially by smaller, entrepreneurial organizations, will lead to increased demand for products and services available by modem. As individuals and companies become even more familiar and comfortable with online communications, usage of the technology for business will increase further.

In addition, with the continuing increase in new business start-ups, there is growth in marketing and printing-related services. Each new business needs printed matter in order to begin operations. And smaller firms will seek out the printer that is the most cost-effective and easiest to work with. Online connections will become inevitable.

The challenge will be to encourage companies to change from delivering materials on disk to transmitting files by modem. In addition, getting ahead and staying ahead of competitors will be a challenge as other firms embrace online technology.

In general, all the information collected here supports the need for less expensive, quality printing services that would be available through online means or through traditional delivery methods.

8

The Least You Need to Know

➤ Although your findings are the most interesting part of a report, how you reached those findings is just as important.

➤ Your findings and report should be objective and based on facts.

➤ Don't state personal opinions or use phrases that suggest you are guessing at what you are reporting.

➤ When making recommendations, think about how your findings affect your company and what the company should do about them.

➤ Use your report as a guide when making verbal presentations. You can create simple overhead transparencies for each major point.

Chapter 22

Press Releases

In This Chapter

➤ The crucial elements of a press release

➤ How to improve your chances of earning publicity

➤ Formatting how-tos

➤ Sample releases

Have you ever noticed how some companies and individuals are constantly being mentioned in the paper or are interviewed on TV? You may wonder how they manage to be quoted everywhere while you're not when you are just as worthy of attention.

Well, don't take it personally. You are probably just as deserving of attention as that media hog, but you aren't going after the attention the way you need to. If you were, you would also be featured in numerous articles or called on to make a commentary on a breaking news story. The problem is that the media doesn't know who you are, how to contact you, or what your area of expertise is.

How to Get Newsworthy Information into the Hands of the Media

In order to put yourself in contention for media coverage, you need to provide editors, reporters, and program managers with the information listed above in the format they want. Which means you need to issue a press release.

Then to keep yourself or your employer in the public eye, you need to make a habit of sending out releases on a regular basis, so that the media gets used to hearing from you. Be careful not to issue releases just for the sake of sending out a mailing; be sure you have something of interest to report or you'll earn a reputation as a time-waster. Like the boy who cried wolf, when you finally have something momentous to proclaim, no one will want to listen. Ask yourself whether the information you're announcing is going to be of interest to anyone and if the answer is "no," hold off on sending it at all.

What Is a Press Release?

A press release is a one to three page document written to announce some newsworthy event or accomplishment to the members of the press. To be useful to the media, your press release must be of potential interest to their readers, viewers, or listeners, and it must be timely.

Tip

Some typical newsworthy events are:

➤ A recent promotion or new position

➤ A speech to be given at a national conference or meeting

➤ Selection for a position on an organization's board of directors

➤ An award or honor

➤ The expansion or planned expansion of your company's facilities

➤ The introduction of a new product or service

➤ The availability of a free newsletter or booklet

➤ A special event, such as a grand opening celebration

There is a set format that the media expects you to follow when sending out a press release, which you'll hear about shortly. If you can make your press release look like the sample releases at the end of the chapter, you're already halfway to getting some publicity.

Once your release has been written, the second challenge is getting it into the hands of the appropriate editor or program manager. Identifying who may be most interested in your information is best accomplished by reading the publications you want to be featured in and noting who's responsible for the section you think is right for your story. Television and radio programs have program managers who decide what stories will be covered and who the guests will be.

> **Tip**
> There are guides available that will give you the names, addresses, and telephone numbers of almost every known reporter. My favorite is *Bacon's Media Directories*, which are reference manuals listing virtually every newspaper, magazine, newsletter, and television and radio show out there. Call them at 800-621-0561 to learn more about their directories.

How Should It Be Written?

When writing a press release, make sure you start with the most important information first. Lead off your first paragraph with a short summary of the announcement. Then provide details in the paragraphs that follow. Prioritize your information and then write it so the crucial points are covered in order of descending importance.

Since editors often have to cut information due to space constraints and since it's easy to edit from the bottom of a release up, it's important to get the critical information in at the beginning of the release. Then if something does have to be cut, it will be one of the less important details at the bottom.

To help you decide which information is considered critical, ask yourself if your press release answers the following six questions: Who?, Where?, What?, Why?, When? and How?

> **Quote**
> Author Marcia Yudkin says the four common deadly mistakes on press releases are:
>
> ➤ Any hint of advertising
>
> ➤ Even a smidgen of hype
>
> ➤ Lack of focus
>
> ➤ Vague characterizations
>
> Marcia Yudkin, author of *Six Steps to Free Publicity*.

Who?

In your release, you may need to provide some background information about a celebrity who is coming to town to perform, or about the new members of the local Rotary club's board of directors or about the individuals who participated in the American Heart Association's annual fund drive that raised $10 million.

Every story has a person or a group of people who need to be mentioned. Even if the subject of your release is not a person, you'll still need to explain who is eligible to audition, attend, or participate in the event you're announcing.

Where?

Always include the street address of the location where your event will take place. If you're announcing the grand opening of a new store on Broad Street, give the exact address, such as 23 Broad Street, Anytown, New York. If you're sending a press release to the local papers in Anytown, you don't need to list the city and state. But if you're sending it out of the area, listing the city and state is a smart idea so there's no confusion.

Even if your press release isn't about a particular event, you'll want to mention where the award ceremony took place, where the new corporate headquarters are to be situated, or, at least, where your company is located.

What?

The "what" of your release is usually the easiest to figure out—it's the reason you're writing the release at all. What happened recently at your organization that everyone wants to hear about? Are you planning a major reorganization? Is the CEO stepping down? Is a new product about to be announced?

Why?

In your release, you'll want to elaborate on the reason for your announcement. Why is a fund raiser being held? Why is the local politician getting an honorary degree? Why is your new product so revolutionary? Provide details to explain how this situation came to be.

When?

In every case, there is a time element that needs to be reported to the media. For instance, if your manufacturing plant recently produced its one millionth widget, you'd want to report how long it took to reach that momentous occasion (ten years? one year? six months?) and on what date the special widget was manufactured.

It's important to be specific about when something will occur or has occurred. If you're planning a concert for this weekend, give the month and date of the concert rather than stating that it will be held "on Saturday at 8:00 pm." If the mail is delayed and the release appears in next week's paper, you'll have a problem on your hands when people show up at the concert hall this Saturday. And there would be no way for the paper to know that you were talking about the previous weekend—unless you give the month and date in addition to the day.

How?

Sometimes determining the "how" element of your release can be a little tricky. Consider these examples to give you some ideas: Suppose an employee at your company has just patented a new product she developed. You'd want to find out how she ever came up with the idea. Or if you're promoting a raffle for your church, you'd want to tell people how they can buy tickets and how much they cost.

Dos and Don'ts

If you follow the standard press release format outlined below, you'll clear one hurdle toward securing media attention. And if you couple that with timely, newsworthy information, you'll have a good shot at earning some publicity for yourself or your organization. Here are some additional dos and don'ts to help you improve your chances for success:

Dos

➤ Do use full names of people and organizations, rather than nicknames or acronyms. Some reporters may not immediately recognize your organization's name if you don't spell it out completely. In addition, if you don't spell out names, you run the risk of having someone on the staff of the newspaper assuming that you're referring to a different company altogether. Don't leave anything open to guessing.

➤ Do allow enough time for the release to reach its intended recipient before the TV or radio show is produced or the publication is printed. If you're sending a press release to a weekly newspaper, keep in mind that the information you're providing probably won't be printed until two to three weeks from the time it is received. So if you're announcing a seminar you're holding in mid-August, the release should be mailed no later than the last week in July.

➤ Do mail the release to a particular person whenever possible. If you don't know the name of the reporter who covers the arts and entertainment section of your local paper and you have an announcement you feel is perfect for that section, just pick up the phone and ask who to send the release to. Try and avoid sending a release to "editor" because the chances of it getting lost in the shuffle are greatly increased. Being able to send a release to a particular person improves the odds that at least it will get read and considered.

Tip
If you'd like to have your photos returned after the publication is through with them, simply put your request on a Post-it™ and stick it on the front of the photo. Also enclose a self-addressed, stamped envelope.

➤ Do send along photographs when appropriate. For instance, when announcing a new hire or promotion at your company, send a 5" × 7" black-and-white headshot with the press release. In general, send black-and-white photos to newspapers (which usually only print using black ink) and ask magazines if they'd prefer color (if they print using color).

Don'ts

➤ Don't send a cover letter with a press release—it's redundant. You should say everything that's considered important in the press release.

➤ Don't allow spelling or grammatical errors to sidetrack your release. Because editors and reporters get hundreds or even thousands of press releases each day, they'll take advantage of any excuse to be able to discard one. If they spot obvious spelling mistakes, your chances for coverage are seriously hampered.

➤ Don't send a release to more than one reporter at a publication, radio, or television station, unless there are writers assigned to different "beats" or areas, such as business, education, and medical. One contact is enough. If one writer decides to cover your story and finds out later that another person on the staff also is covering it, you risk irritating several people.

➤ Don't call a reporter to find out when your "story is going to appear." You're assuming that they even want to write about you, which is dangerous. They're doing you a favor by writing about you or your organization, so don't take up much of their time following up on a press release you sent them.

Formatting How-Tos

No one will argue that what you have to say is more important than how it looks on the page, but when it comes to getting the attention of the media, appropriate formatting is a must. When preparing a press release, be sure to use the following guidelines:

➤ List the name and phone number of a "media contact"—someone a reporter can call for more information. This should be the first item on an 8 1/2 × 11 page, on the upper right-hand side.

➤ Specify when the release can be used. If you don't want the information published before a certain date, type "EMBARGOED UNTIL _____" in all caps on the left-hand side of the page. In most cases, you'll want them to use the information as soon as possible. In this case, type "For Immediate Release" or "Release at Convenience."

➤ The next element is the headline. Determine the most important piece of information in the release and announce it in the next line. "Local Company Reports 100% Growth" would be one potential headline. "ABC Company Hires Ad Executive" would be another. Just focus on the single most important fact in the release and make that your headline.

➤ Below the headline is the beginning of the release. Type the city name where the release is being issued, then a comma, then the two-letter state abbreviation, followed by the month and day of the year. To separate this information from the actual start of the release, type two hyphens "--."

➤ The entire release should be typed, double-spaced, with margins of one inch all the way around.

➤ Many releases will be just one page long, but if yours needs to continue onto another page, type "More" and center it at the bottom of the page. This alerts editors that there is more information to follow on the next page.

➤ At the end of the release, type "###" or "End" and center it below the last sentence. This is also a signal that there is no additional information.

➤ Send the release out on your organization's letterhead. This helps immediately identify who is providing the information.

Sample Releases

To get you started in putting together your own press release, following are a few samples:

PERSONNEL ANNOUNCEMENT

Media contact:
Susan Lewis
415-555-1234
FAX: 415-555-1233

FOR IMMEDIATE RELEASE

MERGERS AND ACQUISITIONS SPECIALIST

JOINS SMITH LAW FIRM

San Francisco, CA, April 14 -- Alan Jones, an experienced business and securities lawyer formerly based in Chicago has joined the Smith Law Firm as counsel.

After more than 25 years of experience serving U.S. and international small and middle market corporations, Mr. Jones has become affiliated with the Smith Law Firm of San Francisco. His practice emphasizes mergers and acquisitions, joint ventures, licensing, distribution and financing transactions for clients in the U.S. and abroad.

Before joining the Smith Law Firm, Mr. Jones was a partner with Jones & Jones, a partner with Newman & Newman, and an associate with Black, Levinson and Doe, all in Chicago.

Mr. Jones is a member of the Small Business Committee of the American Bar Association, which studies legal issues related to small business management. He has also been published in the Review of International Affairs.

Mr. Jones received his law degree from Harvard Law School and his undergraduate degree from Columbia University.

The Smith Law Firm focuses on helping the owners and managers of small and mid-sized companies. They are located at 1 Big Firm Road, San Francisco, California.

BOARD OF DIRECTORS ANNOUNCEMENT

Media contact:
Kathy Clark
President, NAWBO
222-1111

FOR IMMEDIATE RELEASE

NAWBO ELECTS NEW OFFICERS AND BOARD OF DIRECTORS

Roch., NY, June 13 -- The Rochester Chapter of the National Association of Women Business Owners has elected new officers and a new board of directors for 1994-1995.

The new chapter officers are:

President-Kathy Clark of Clark Moving & Storage

President-elect-Julia Garver of Woods, Oviatt, Gilman, Sturman & Clarke

Treasurer-Patricia O'May of Business Systems Management

Secretary-Roslyn Bakst Goldman, appraiser and fine art consultant

The new board of directors and their respective committee responsibilities are:

Communications committee-Marjorie Crum of Happy Creek Studio

Community liaison committee-Valerie Mannix of Mercury Print Productions

Corporate committee and past-president-Eileen Coyle of Monroe Ambulance

Government affairs committee-Tracey Long of Long & Associates

Marketing committee-Elizabeth Thorley of IDS Financial Services

Membership committee-Sharon Stiller of Underberg & Kessler

Program committee-Marjorie Wiseman, CLU

At-large member-Lorraine Wolch, CPA, PC

The National Association of Women Business Owners, headquartered in Chicago, is the only dues-based national organization representing the interests of all women entrepreneurs. Membership is open to sole proprietors, partners, and corporate owners with day-to-day management responsibility.

###

NEW PRODUCT/SERVICE ANNOUNCEMENT

Media contact:
Joan Smith
Waterstreet Graphics
Phone: 800-555-5555
FAX: 716-555-5556

FOR IMMEDIATE USE

WATERSTREET GRAPHICS FIRST FIRM IN REGION

TO OFFER LARGE FORMAT COLOR PRINTING

WEBSTER, NY, September 27 -- Waterstreet Graphics in Webster is the first firm in the state outside New York City to install a Xerox color printing system that allows the company to provide full color, large format printed products in virtually any size. These products include display and presentation materials, trade show graphics, backlit displays, posters, and signage.

"We see some of the largest opportunities in the retail industry," says Waterstreet Graphics President Paul Romeo, "where announcements of sales or store specials require constantly changing signage. We can provide a full color poster or banner customized for each store that uses the same image but with varying text. All for very reasonable prices."

Never before has it been possible to apply text directly onto a color image and print it for such a reasonable price. Waterstreet Graphics can now provide print quantities as small as 1 or as many as 500 at prices well below current methods, which are photographic-based. Turnaround time is available in hours instead of days. Prints can be made in sizes up to 42 inches wide and up to 500 feet long.

–MORE–

Waterstreet Graphics/Page 2

Trade show organizers, advertising agencies, marketing communications profession-als, architects, map makers, sign manufacturers, and graphic designers are already using the service.

Images can be taken from a variety of media including photographs, negatives and transparencies, computer disks, or CD-ROM.

"Xerox wide format digital color printing systems offer a variety of new business opportunities for many of our customers," said Paul V. Cahn, vice president of market-ing, Xerox Engineering Systems. "We're excited about having Waterstreet Graphics as a Xerox customer and provider of these printing services.

–END–

The Least You Need to Know

➤ Make sure you explain the who, why, what, when, where, and how of your announcement.

➤ Make sure to send your press release to the appropriate person. Use a media guide to find names and addresses.

➤ Allow enough time for your release to get to the recipient.

➤ By using the standard format for a press release, you significantly improve your chances of gaining publicity.

Chapter 23

Editor Query Letters

In This Chapter

➤ Editor query letters vs. press releases

➤ How to write a query letter that'll get noticed

➤ Press kits—getting to know you

➤ Sample letters

Press releases are perfect for making announcements and reporting success, but in many cases, you may have a story to tell that just isn't right for a press release. If you'd like to propose writing a column for a magazine or submitting an article on a timely topic, a press release wouldn't be the right tool to use. In these cases, when you want to propose that a particular article be written—either about you or by you—you should send an editor query letter.

Definition

Editor Query Letter   A one to two page letter sent to a writer, editor, or broadcast program manager suggesting that a particular story be given coverage. You are "querying" the editor to gauge his or her interest in your article idea.

Selling an Editor on a Story

Some people refer to editor query letters as "editor pitch letters" because your purpose is to "pitch" or propose a certain story or angle. You're trying to persuade an editor that your topic is worthy of coverage. The advantage of proposing an article that you write yourself is that you can guide the content to cover the issues you feel are most important, rather than having someone else report on what he sees as most relevant. However, even if a staff reporter writes the piece, you can still shape how the article is written by suggesting a particular angle or perspective.

Ultimately, the goal of each query letter is to have an article appear in a publication that benefits you or the organization you represent.

Why Write a Query Letter

There are several reasons why you should write a query letter to an editor:

➤ If you're trying to obtain publicity for yourself or an organization you're associated with

➤ If you're a freelance writer interested in being hired to write an article

Definition
Byline Information listed either above or below an article indicating the author's name. Getting credit for articles you've written is an important step if you're at all interested in a writing career.

➤ If you want to write an article in return for a byline in the publication so you can gain credibility as a writer or improve your professional visibility

A press release is designed to announce a piece of news to the media in the most efficient way possible; this is why you can write one press release and mail it to numerous editors. However, the whole point of a query letter is to customize your article proposal to that particular editor, publication, and readership. Each letter will need to be different, highlighting certain aspects of your background that may be of interest to some magazines but not others, or focusing on an element that one newspaper has written about recently.

Tip

Once you've identified a particular publication in which you'd like to be featured, pick a column or department where your article would be most appropriate. Then address your query letter to the writer or reporter responsible for that section. Often getting your idea into the right hands is half the battle of obtaining publicity.

How to Write a Letter That Gets Results

Although each letter you write will be different, since you're sending it to different editors, there are common pieces of information that you need to cover in each and every letter. Here is a format to guide you:

Paragraph 1

In the first paragraph, introduce yourself. If you are a subscriber or regular reader of the publication, mention that.

Paragraph 2

In the next paragraph, propose your article idea. In two to three sentences, describe what exactly you want the article to be about, why it will be of interest to the publication's target audience, and in what ways it will benefit the reader. If the article is related to a recent event, trend, or report, mention how your article furthers that discussion.

For instance, say you're a doctor who has found that eating a certain type of vegetable significantly reduces cholesterol. You could point out that your findings support the notion that diet has a lot to do with cholesterol levels. And you can also claim that your research now gives people some specific actions they can take to control cholesterol—eating more of this vegetable.

Paragraph 3

Following that information, if you are proposing to write the article, explain why you are qualified to write on the topic. Briefly detail your background, experience, and knowledge of the subject you want to write about.

Paragraph 4

Wrap up your letter by thanking the recipient for considering your request. If you intend to follow up (which isn't recommended for the very large publications), state when you'll call.

Dos and Don'ts

Although writing an editor query letter is similar to writing a sales letter, there are some specific guidelines to follow when drafting your pitch.

Dos

➤ Do try to keep the length to one page. Editors are busy people who prefer to receive letters that get right to the point. You should strive to make your case in 4–5 paragraphs.

➤ Do compliment the editor or reporter on previous articles she has written that you read and liked. But be genuine. If you've never read the reporter's pieces, don't lie.

➤ Do suggest a specific type of article or topic, rather than just asking to have an article written about you or your company. Tell them briefly why they should write about you.

➤ Do provide a few sentences of background information on who you are, what's remarkable about you or your company, and how the article you're suggesting relates to your business. (For example, make sure to mention you're a business attorney if you're proposing to write about the new Limited Liability Company structure).

Definition
Press Kit A pocket folder containing background information on an organization to help editors better understand what a company does. Usually a press release related to the pitch letter is also included, as well as a few recent clippings from other articles.

➤ Do specifically ask that an article be written. Don't be wishy-washy or unclear when it comes to telling the editor what you want. But keep in mind that you're asking for a favor of sorts, so don't be too pushy.

➤ Do send along a press kit or a packet of background material if it supports your pitch.

➤ Do send your query letter on your organization's letterhead if the article idea relates to them. And if it's an idea unrelated to your employer, send it on personal stationery instead.

Don'ts

➤ Don't send clippings of other articles that are identical to what you want this publisher to print. No one wants to be perceived as a copycat. But related clippings are OK.

➤ Don't bring up whether you are an advertiser in the publication or not, or try to use that to your advantage. Publications keep their advertising and editorial departments quite separate and are offended if you suggest that you can buy yourself some coverage.

➤ Don't send an article that you've already written along with your query. If the editor is interested in your idea, he'll let you know and tell you how he wants it written. If you send one that's already completed, you run the risk of having it tossed out because it wasn't exactly what was wanted. By sending the letter alone, you give the editorial staff the opportunity to make modifications to your idea that suit them. Then when they let you know that they want you to write the article, you can write it with their directions in mind.

What Your Query Letter Should Look Like

A query letter is formatted just like all your other business letters. The most common form is the block layout, which is formatted this way:

Date

Address of intended recipient

Dear _____,

First paragraph—Introduce yourself and your article idea.

Second paragraph—Elaborate a little on why the idea is interesting.

Third paragraph—Explain why you are the perfect person to write it.

Fourth paragraph—Mention that you're enclosing writing samples and ask the editor to consider your idea.

Closing,

Your name and title

Tip

Items you should include in your press kit are:

➤ A timely press release

➤ A black-and-white photo (of a person, product, building, or event depending on what the query letter proposes)

➤ Press clippings from previous articles (2–3 is sufficient)

➤ A fact sheet containing basic information about the product, company or person

➤ A resume or bio page if the query letter is in regards to an individual

Sample Query Letters

Use the following samples to get you started in writing your own query letters. These are all actual letters that have been used to pursue publicity.

FOR A NATIONAL FEATURE ARTICLE ABOUT YOUR COMPANY

April 28, 1993

Tanya Trowell
Editorial Assistant
Home Office Computing
730 Broadway
New York, NY 10003

Dear Ms. Trowell:

I've enjoyed your writing for the "Pro File" section of *Home Office Computing* and wondered whether you might consider covering my firm, Layton & Co., in a future issue.

Layton & Co. is a business that has grown from a part-time operation (while I worked at a full-time corporate job) to a rapidly expanding national business plan writing service. And because such a large proportion of your readership is running a business part-time or thinking about starting a business, they might find some useful insights from editorial coverage of my firm's growth.

My firm works almost exclusively with small and start-up businesses, providing business plan writing services. What I offer is the expertise to translate an entrepreneur's vision and business goals into a clear plan to be used in securing financing. I am currently working with several local and national clients to develop effective business plans and secure funding.

So that you can evaluate whether my business would be appropriate for your section, I've enclosed an information packet on my services. I also have a number of clients who would be happy to comment on the value of using a business plan writer to complete a plan, should you be interested in their perspective.

Thank you for your time. Please feel free to contact me at any time. I look forward to reading more of your work in future issues of *Home Office Computing*.

Best regards,

Marcia Layton

Enclosure

FOR A LOCAL FEATURE ARTICLE ABOUT YOUR COMPANY

June 12, 1995

Mary Morgan
Rochester Business Journal
55 St. Paul Street
Rochester, NY 14604

Dear Mary,

As a *Rochester Business Journal* subscriber, I read your profiles in the "Enterprise" section regularly. And I was wondering whether you would consider covering my business, MAC'S Automotive, in an upcoming column.

MAC'S Automotive provides top quality auto collision and repair service. But what really sets us apart, aside from some of the best mechanics and technicians in Rochester, is the extent to which we go to care for our customers.

We recognize that being without a car can be an extremely inconvenient time, so we work to provide state-of-the-art technology to keep customers in touch with us and with others. This includes supplying customers with pagers and cellular phones. We also provide shuttle service to and from work for customers who drop their car off at our shop here on Seneca Avenue.

We regularly survey customers to find out how we're doing in terms of meeting their needs, and we consistently hear back that we're doing very well.

In addition to performing repair work on cars, we have also recently become certified to perform boat repairs. At this time of year, local boat owners may be interested to learn of our services.

I'd certainly enjoy the opportunity to provide you with additional information on my company, if you're interested. Please feel free to call me at 555-1234 to discuss this or to ask any questions about MAC'S Automotive.

Thank you for your time. I look forward to reading more of your articles in the *Rochester Business Journal*.

Sincerely yours,

Michael Bartikofsky
President

FOR INCLUSION AS A GUEST ON A RADIO SHOW

July 10, 1995

Olivia Bradford
WGUN
2901 Mountain Industrial Blvd.
Tucker, GA 30083

Dear Ms. Bradford,

I noted with interest the information in this week's "PartyLine" regarding your program, "Talk for Women" and wanted to pitch having me as a guest on your show.

As a woman business owner, I am very much aware of the lack of information available for other women entrepreneurs. In my business as a PR and business writing consultant, I advise business owners nationwide on how to increase their presence in the media. And I'd like the chance to discuss "How to Get More Publicity for Your Business" with your guests.

My clients and my own firm have achieved remarkable increases in sales, inquiries, and awareness through simple yet effective steps to getting more media exposure. Whether your listeners are involved in running a business or in volunteer and non-profit organizations of any kind, they will find my advice practical and immediately useful.

I have a tape of a recent one-hour radio show I did on the topic of women business owners and the challenge of personal financial planning that I'd be happy to send you.

I look forward to hearing from you if you'd like to discuss having me appear as a guest on your show. Thank you for your consideration.

Best regards,

Sue Smith

The Least You Need to Know

➤ Use an editor query letter to propose an article that you'd like to write or have written.

➤ Be as persuasive as possible in preferably one page.

➤ Send your letter to the editor or writer responsible for the section of the publication in which you want to appear.

➤ Compile a press kit to accompany your letter.

Chapter 24

Writing an Article and Getting It Published

In This Chapter

➤ What you need to know before you begin writing

➤ Why writing for free isn't so bad

➤ Paid assignments vs. freebies

➤ How to improve your odds of getting published

Are you interested in seeing your name in print? While many people believe that getting published is quite a feat, the truth is that it's not as hard as you might think. The first step is getting an editor interested in what you want to write about. And you've already learned how to write a query letter in Chapter 23. So to get over the next hurdle, you just need to start writing.

Questions You Need Answered First

Once you receive word from an editor that she is interested in your article idea, you'll want to find out as much as possible about what she expects to receive from you. This means you'll want to ask the following:

➤ How long should the article be? This is usually measured in the number of words, rather than pages.

➤ Are you expected to supply photos, or will a staff photographer or artist take care of this?

➤ Are there particular aspects of your article that should be emphasized or explored? For example, if you're going to write about telecommuting (where employees work from home and keep in touch with their businesses via telephone, email, or fax), should you concentrate on the technical demands of setting up a telecommuting situation, or on case histories of various telecommuters?

Definition

Case History   An example or story about a person or company. Also called "case studies," these anecdotes can be part of an article, or can be an article on their own. Typical case studies are about clients who use a company's products and the benefits they experienced from them.

➤ How many people should be quoted in the article, if any? Some publications require that at least three people be interviewed to give their opinions or perspectives on a topic, while others leave that decision to the writer.

Tip
Whenever you submit a photo, make sure you identify who or what is in the picture. Write a description on a sticky label and place it on the back of the photo. This way, if your photo gets separated from the rest of your material, someone will be able to identify it.

➤ Are there specific people who need to be interviewed? In some instances, the opinions and data from experts in a particular field are needed to simply give your article credibility.

➤ What kind of byline will you get? Some publications list only the author's full name while others provide one to two sentences at the end of a piece about the author's background. Of course the more information given about you, the better.

➤ Will a small photo of you accompany the article? A few publications show a headshot of the author next to the byline. Since name (and face) recognition is hard to get, send a black-and-white glossy ASAP if it will be printed.

Are You Writing for Fame or Fortune?

You may decide to try writing to gain exposure for yourself or your organization. Publicity can do a number of things:

➤ Promote yourself or your company

➤ Establish credibility

➤ Promote a product or service in order to generate sales

➤ Increase familiarity with your company

➤ Alert customers to new ways they can use your product

Or, you can try writing as a means to generate income. However, if you don't have a track record of writing for other publications, it will be difficult at first for you to earn paid writing assignments. You may ask why would you ever offer to write an article for free. The answer is that many magazines and newspapers will take a chance on you for free even if you don't have much experience.

Whether your goal is simply to get some free publicity or to become a freelance writer, you'll need to begin collecting several samples of your writing that have been published. The easiest and fastest way to do this is to offer your writing talents for free at first. Remember, you've got to start somewhere. Then after you have a portfolio of clippings, you can start sending query letters to editors regarding paid assignments.

While the process of writing an article is much the same whether you do it for publicity or for money, there are different guidelines for each that will be discussed later.

Your Article Options

We've been talking about writing an article as if there were just one type. In reality there are several varieties of articles each containing its own length, tone, and purpose:

Column   A series of articles generally on the same subject, such as marketing or art, which is often based on the writer's personal experience or training.

Case history   An example story showcasing the effects of a product or the use of an organization on an individual or group. A story about how one non-profit organization saved thousands of dollars by following the advice of a particular accounting firm would be an example of a case history.

Expertise article   A piece that informs the audience how to do something better, based on the author's personal expertise, or explains a topic that the writer is qualified to write about. For example, an article about trends in online marketing could be written by an online service provider or by a computer consultant.

Opinion   In most newspapers, there is a section for people to express their opinions on virtually any subject they want. Frequently the topics are related to local government, recent news reports, or controversial proposals. Many of these articles are written by average citizens who just want to speak their minds. You should find this section as an opportunity to get your opinion published too. Of course, you'll need to submit your article to the editor first for review and selection, but it is easier to have an article published in this area than almost any other.

> **Tip**
> Industry trade journals (publications written for a specific market such as *Computer Reseller News* and *Underhood Service*) are often more receptive to publishing articles from outsiders—people who aren't on their editorial staff.

Profile   A detailed description of a person or organization. It should include enough information so that readers feel that they know the person better after reading your article.

Getting Down to Writing

The hardest part of writing an article is leading it off with just the right angle. Keep in mind that you want to include just the right amount of information to entice the reader to want to read more. A lot depends on what you write in the first paragraph—even the first sentence.

To get yourself going, focus on the main point you want to make in your article. What information do you want readers to leave with? Sometimes starting an article with a question to draw readers in is a good strategy. The rest of your article can then focus on answering the question. For example, an article on writing a business plan might begin with the question: "Do you have a written business plan?" Then you can proceed to tell readers why they should have a plan and how they can write one.

Another tactic is to start with a quotation that summarizes the point you are trying to make. Then you can explain what the author meant by the quote and go on to say whether you agree or disagree with him.

At one point or another, we were all taught the inverted pyramid technique of writing; starting with general information and working down to more specific data. You can use this technique to outline your thoughts, or you can turn the pyramid upside down—that is, start with a specific claim and then elaborate on it in your article.

No matter which method you choose to begin your article, make sure each point you make in it logically follows the previous one. Before you begin to write, take notes on every major point you want to get across to the reader. Then rearrange these points into an order that contains an introduction, supporting information, and a conclusion that pulls everything together.

If you're writing something that has a time element, it may make sense to organize your information chronologically. Then tell your story in the order in which it happened.

Don't get hung up on individual words as you write your first draft, just pretend you are talking to a friend. Explain what you are trying to communicate to your friend, even if she's not in the room. Sometimes talking out loud helps us figure out the best way to express something.

It's All in the Name

After you've written your article, you'll want to come up with a snappy title that makes people want to read it. The best headlines sum up what's in the body of the article while catching the reader's interest. Don't worry about the length of the title: sometimes the longer ones are better because they completely explain why someone should read the article.

Titles with numbers in them are effective, such as "Seven tips for improving your time management skills" or "Ten ways to save over $1,000 this year."

Emphasizing the benefits of your article is the best way to come up with a title. What exactly are readers going to learn from your article? What are they going to get out of it? Once you reread your article and try to answer these questions in a few words—you'll have the beginning of your title.

Dos and Don'ts of Getting Published

Getting your article written is your first challenge; getting it published is your second. Use the following suggestions to improve your odds of getting published:

Dos

➤ Do send out editor pitch letters before you start writing, rather than the other way around. You'll save time and energy by first determining which publications might want to publish your piece. Since each newspaper and magazine have different writing styles, article lengths, and preferences, it's wise to find out what their needs are before you finalize your masterpiece. If you don't, you may find yourself spending a lot of time editing later.

➤ Do offer diagrams, illustrations, and photos to supplement your article. Sometimes a picture really clarifies a point you've tried to make in your writing, so think about what visual aids you could offer to go along with your piece.

➤ Do refer to other articles the publication has already printed as a guide to how you should write. Scanning past articles will tell you whether you should write in first, second, or third person, how long the article should be, and what kinds of visuals are typically used.

Tip

Request that publications send you their "writer's guidelines" which outline what they expect to see in terms of style, length, tone, and format. Usually these are free. However if you also want a sample issue, you'll have to pay the cover price.

Don'ts

➤ Don't write an article that is completely self-promotional. Even if you're writing an article about your company's product, make sure your statements are based on fact and not on opinion.

➤ Don't exaggerate or you'll lose credibility. Your chances of getting published will increase if you write like an unbiased reporter doing a story.

➤ Don't let spelling or grammatical errors throw you off course. Even if you've written the best article, poor spelling, punctuation, or grammatical goofs may cause editors to put your article aside rather than print it.

➤ Don't write in the first person unless the editor requests it, such as in the case of an expertise article where your observations are based on your own experience. Even if you have to refer to yourself in your article, try and rewrite it so that you don't overuse "me," "myself," or "I."

Design and Formatting

How you format an article depends on whether you're being paid to write it or not. If you are being paid, there are strict guidelines you'll have to follow. If you're writing for free, you're given more leeway in how the article should look on paper.

The Freebie

Since you're providing something for free that newspapers and magazines often have to pay for, there are only a few rules you'll have to follow when formatting your article.

However, it is helpful to editors when you do the following:

➤ Provide both a printout of your article on plain white paper *and* a computer disk with the file on it (you'll need to find out whether they want a PC- or Macintosh-formatted version).

➤ Double-space everything. This gives the editor space to make notes and changes right on the pages.

➤ Give your article a title and type it at the beginning of the piece.

➤ Type your name either directly below the title, or at the very end of the article. If you are permitted to write a couple of sentences describing who you are, do that at the end of the piece.

Tip
The Writer's Digest Guide to Manuscript Formats can show you how professional writers are expected to submit articles they've written for pay. If you're unclear on how an editor wants your article to look, just ask and they'll tell you their formatting requirements.

Tip
When you mention the name of the company you work for at the end of your article, also state what the company does and what your title is there. This is important especially if the name doesn't exactly make it clear what the company does. For example, "Bob Smith is Vice President of Marketing at Jones & Associates, a distributor of vitamins and health products."

➤ Number the pages.

➤ Type either your last name or the title of the article in the top left-hand corner of each page. This way, if the pages get mixed up, they can be reassembled in the correct order.

The Purchased Piece

Yes, you're being paid to write. That's the great news. And with that honor comes some higher expectations for how you'll submit your articles. Here are instructions from *The Writer's Digest Guide to Manuscript Formats* for formatting your article:

➤ Always double-space your articles.

➤ On the first page of your article, write the number of words in the piece in the upper right-hand corner of the page.

249

➤ Move down one-third of the page and type the title of the article in the center of the page.

➤ Directly underneath the title, write your name—for example, "By John Q. Public."

➤ Indent each new paragraph.

➤ Number each page in the bottom center.

➤ In the upper left-hand corner of each page following the first page, type your last name and a mini-headline for the article. For example, "Sutton/Direct mail."

➤ If you're allowed to provide some information about your background, write that at the end of the piece.

➤ Type "End" at the conclusion of the article.

Remember, when a publication hires you to write an article, they exert a lot more control over how the article is written and how it is formatted. Make sure to follow these steps since editors expect that you will.

Samples

Sick Building Syndrome
By Ron Maier

Although virtually unheard of a decade ago, sick building syndrome has become a major issue for many employees, employers, and building owners. It is a disorder caused by inadequate ventilation and filtration in a building, trapping pollutants, toxins from man-made fibers in carpeting and paint, second-hand smoke, viruses, bacteria and residue from modern building materials within buildings. Poor indoor air quality exposes 60 to 120 million people a year to contaminants that make them sick, according to Professor James E. Woods of Virginia Polytechnic Institute. And it costs employers an estimated $60 billion annually in lost productivity and worker illness...

Ron Maier is president of KENRON INDUSTRIAL AIR CONDITIONING, INC. in Rochester. KENRON specializes in treating poor indoor air quality and sick building syndrome.

An expertise article should be approximately 1,600 words.

What Exactly Is a Marketing Plan?

While most entrepreneurs recognize the importance of marketing, few take the time to actually write a marketing plan. Many don't feel it necessary to commit their plan to paper, preferring instead to work from ideas in their head. But the act of writing out a marketing strategy has been proven to significantly increase the odds of actually making it happen....

Marcia Layton owns Layton & Co., marketing and public relations consultants. She can be reached at 716-555-5555.

A column.

The best he could:
Vietnam vet fought to live until war caught up to him
By Maria Justice

As I entered the house with post-Christmas sales packages, my son said hurriedly, "Dad is on the phone. He's been calling you."

"What's up?" I asked with an exhausted voice.

"It's David, the vet...someone has been trying to reach you. It doesn't sound good."

David, a Vietnam War veteran, had committed suicide. It was only a matter of time. He had tried before to kill himself, attempts precipitated by the emotional scars of the war...

Justice, of Hilton, is a case manager at The Health Association and she serves on the board of the Veterans Outreach Center.

An opinion/editorial piece.

Since the early 1980s, Kodak has worked with Hughes and Luce, serving their copying needs with 18 Ektaprint 235 copiers, two Ektaprint 300 copiers, and two Ektaprint 90 copiers.

But last year, when Hughes and Luce hired a new executive director, it was unclear whether the lease on the firm's Kodak copiers would be renewed. The new director, John Adrian, came from a leading San Francisco law firm in which only Xerox copiers were used....

A case history.

The Least You Need to Know

➤ There are several types of articles: case histories, expertise articles, columns, opinion-editorials, and profiles.

➤ Ask questions and request a copy of the publication's writer's guidelines before you begin to write.

➤ If your long-term goal is to be a freelance writer, you need to gather several published samples. The simplest way to do this is to write for free at first.

➤ Writers who are paid for articles are expected to follow different standards than those who write for free.

Bibliography

Berger, Arthur Asa, *Improving Writing Skills; Memos, Letters, Reports, and Proposals*, SAGE Publications: CA, 1993

Bowman, Joel P., and Bernadine Branchaw, *How to Write Proposals That Produce*, Oryx Press, AZ, 1992

Brill, Laura, *Business Writing Quick & Easy*, 2nd ed., AMACOM: NY, 1989

Brock, Susan L., *Better Business Writing*, Crisp Publications: CA, 1987

Davidson, Eleanor J., PhD, *Business Writing at Work*, Irwin Mirror Press: IL, 1994

Davidson, Wilma, EdD, *Business Writing: What Works, What Won't*, St. Martin's Press: NY, 1994

Gootnick, David and Margaret Mary Gootnick, eds., *The Standard Handbook of Business Communication*, The Free Press: NY, 1984

Holtz, Herman, *The Independent Consultant's Brochure and Letter Handbook*, John Wiley & Sons, Inc.: NY, 1995

Mundis, Jerrold, *Break Writer's Block Now!*, St. Martin's Press: NY, 1991

Words for the Wise

Bias   Having a preference for something, which then puts another group, idea, or project at a disadvantage.

Bullet Points   Little round dots that appear before sentences. They look like this • and are often used in place of numbers or hyphens.

Byline   Information listed either above or below an article indicating the author's name.

Call to Action   A phrase used in the advertising industry that refers to what you want your sales prospects to do to move the sale forward.

Carbon Copy   This means that you'll send copies of the same memo to other people. Others who will receive a copy are listed after the "cc:" symbol, which stands for carbon copy.

Case History   An example or story about a person or company. Also called "case studies," these anecdotes can be part of an article, or can be the article on its own.

Chart   A diagram used to display information in terms of lines and points on a piece of paper or computer screen.

Colloquial   An informal conversational style that is generally not appropriate for business documents.

Contraction   When two words are joined together to form one, with some letters eliminated in the process. An apostrophe is placed wherever the letters are removed.

Copy Notation   When you need to send a copy of your letter to other people, use the symbol "cc:" at the bottom of your letter to indicate that other people are receiving it, and then list their names in alphabetical order.

Editor Query Letter   A one to two page letter sent to a writer, editor, or broadcast program manager suggesting that a particular story be given coverage. In it you either offer to supply the publication with a specific article that you would write or ask the editor if his publication would consider writing about you or your company. You are "querying" the editor to gauge his interest in your article idea.

Email   Electronic mail. An email message is simply a typed note that is sent through your computer to someone else. In order to transmit the message, your computer must be connected to a modem.

Endnotes   Footnote references that are listed together at the end of a report, rather than within the document.

Font   A term for what the letters on your computer or typewriter look like. There are thousands of different fonts, or *typestyles*, that affect how large or small the letters are, whether they are simple or fancy, and the image they project.

Graphics   Symbols and visual elements that help break up a document. Graphs, charts, illustrations, photographs, and typographical symbols, such as bullet points, are all graphics.

Heading   The title of the section that appears at the beginning of the line. You can have several different levels of headings, corresponding to the various levels of detail in your outline.

Justification   Refers to how elements are aligned on the page. Left justified means that everything is lined up on the left, with the right side of the page remaining jagged. Other options are right justified, centered, and justified (which means that the typing on both sides of the page is straight, not jagged).

Modem   A small device that links your computer to telephone lines, which carry your email messages to other computers hooked up to a modem. You can buy a computer with an "internal modem," or you can purchase an "external modem" that just plugs into your computer and a phone jack.

Online Service   A computer network that has been set by a for-profit company to allow users to send and receive email messages, and search for information such as recent magazine articles and stock performance.

Portfolio   A collection of samples of an artist's best work. A portfolio should show you a wide range of styles and client work so that you get a good feel for how the artist would approach your situation.

Prejudice   Feelings of resentment or dislike for a particular group of people or idea that are generally not based on fact or personal experience.

Press Kit   A pocket folder containing background information on an organization to help editors better understand what a company does. Usually a press release related to the pitch letter is also included, as well as a few recent clippings from other articles.

Random Sample   A research practice that involves selecting research participants at random, rather than choosing specific people for one reason or another. Your research results are considered more accurate and reliable (believable) with random sampling.

Request For Proposal (RFP)   A document prepared by an organization looking to hire a company to provide specific goods or services. The RFP outlines exactly what the company wants to purchase and why, and asks potential suppliers to respond within a certain period of time with a bid.

Sans Serif Typeface   One of the two varieties of lettering used in typed documents. This typeface does not have any extra curves or lines (for example, Helvetica and Futura fonts).

Serif Typeface   One of the two varieties of lettering used in typed documents. The extra lines that extend from the bottom and top of each character give this typeface a fancier look (similar computer fonts are Times and Palatino).

Smileys   Symbols used in electronic communication to help replace facial gestures you normally see when talking directly to someone. They help communicate someone's mood, or indicate when someone's joking.

Synopsis   An overview of the whole proposal.

Tickler   A type of file that consists of 31 days and 12 months, so you can put a note or reminder in a specific future month or daily file to remind you to do something. It's a very helpful follow-up system.

Typographical Errors   Mistakes that are made in using a typewriter or keyboard to type a document.

Writer's Block   An inability to get started, or to continue, with the process of working on a written project, such as an article, memo, letter, or proposal. The feeling of not being able to find the words to express whatever it is that needs to be expressed. If you don't address the situation you can waste considerable time and cause yourself unnecessary stress.

Index